Practical Open Source Software
for Libraries

CHANDOS
INFORMATION PROFESSIONAL SERIES

Series Editor: Ruth Rikowski
(email: Rikowskigr@aol.com)

Chandos' new series of books are aimed at the busy information professional. They have been specially commissioned to provide the reader with an authoritative view of current thinking. They are designed to provide easy-to-read and (most importantly) practical coverage of topics that are of interest to librarians and other information professionals. If you would like a full listing of current and forthcoming titles, please visit our website www.chandospublishing.com or email info@chandospublishing.com or telephone +44 (0) 1223 891358.

New authors: we are always pleased to receive ideas for new titles; if you would like to write a book for Chandos, please contact Dr Glyn Jones on email gjones@chandospublishing.com or telephone number +44 (0) 1993 848726.

Bulk orders: some organisations buy a number of copies of our books. If you are interested in doing this, we would be pleased to discuss a discount. Please email info@chandospublishing.com or telephone +44 (0) 1223 891358.

Practical Open Source Software for Libraries

NICOLE C. ENGARD

Chandos Publishing

Oxford · Cambridge · New Delhi

Chandos Publishing
TBAC Business Centre
Avenue 4
Station Lane
Witney
Oxford OX28 4BN
UK
Tel: +44 (0) 1993 848726
Email: info@chandospublishing.com
www.chandospublishing.com

Chandos Publishing is an imprint of Woodhead Publishing Limited

Woodhead Publishing Limited
Abington Hall
Granta Park
Great Abington
Cambridge CB21 6AH
UK
www.woodheadpublishing.com

First published in 2010

ISBN:
978 1 84334 585 5

© N. C. Engard, 2010

British Library Cataloguing-in-Publication Data.
A catalogue record for this book is available from the British Library.

Typeset by Domex e-Data Pvt. Ltd.
Printed in the UK and USA.

To Chris for being my open source mentor and
to the entire Koha Community for fostering
my love of open source

Contents

List of figures and tables

Figures

Tables

Foreword

When I first corresponded with Nicole, she was a recent library school graduate working at a law library in Philadelphia. She was already aware of the technical merits of free software (as in freedom) and open source software (FOSS) and had redesigned and built the intranet at her work with FOSS tools. What she was only just learning about was the philosophy behind free software. A functioning free and open source software project is about far more than the program code alone; it is as much about freedom and community as it is about software.

The Free Software project I work on – Koha (*http://koha-community.org*), which is an integrated library system – is a good illustration of this community in effect. The fact that a programmer in Poland working for a small monastery can add a feature that makes the lives of the librarians at the Cook Islands National Library better daily is what FOSS is all about. Nicole being a librarian was quick to understand the power of being autonomous and the beauty of a functioning free and open source software project. Indeed one could say the primary function of a librarian is to facilitate the transfer of knowledge, thus empowering their communities, which is the same role free software plays.

In the few short years I have been fortunate to count Nicole as a friend, I have watched her grow from initiate to an integral and indispensable part of a free software project. She runs workshops on open source, gives presentations, blogs almost daily and now writes books on the subject. Her insatiable appetite for knowledge and her desire to make the world a better place make her an excellent teacher; her enthusiasm rubs off on all those around her.

In this book, which is almost like her journey, Nicole takes us through learning what open source is, and tells us what it isn't by examining and debunking some of the more popular myths around it. The book then leads into how libraries can make the best use of open source, with chapters packed full of concrete and real world examples. Each chapter builds on the rest and by the end you will come away with a much deeper understanding of what FOSS is, and why we love it so.

Chris Cormack

Christopher Cormack has a BSc in Computer Science and a BA in Mathematics and Maori Studies. While working for Katipo Communications he was the lead developer of the original version of Koha, which went live at Horowhenua Library Trust on January 5, 2000. Since then he has served various roles in the community as release manager, QA manager and currently translation manager. Christopher believes in free software, and allowing users the freedom to innovate.

About the author

Nicole C. Engard is the Director of Open Source Education at ByWater Solutions. She directs the company's open source education endeavors. In addition to her daily responsibilities, Nicole keeps the library community up to date on web technologies via her website, 'What I Learned Today...' (*http://www.web2learning.net*).

Nicole's interest in library technology started at the Jenkins Law Library in Philadelphia where she worked as the Web Manager. In addition to her web development experiences, Nicole has worked as a Metadata Librarian and librarian trainer. For her innovative uses of technology in libraries, Nicole was named one of Library Journal's Movers & Shakers in 2007.

Nicole received her BA in Literary Studies and Computer Programming from Juniata College in Huntingdon, PA, and her MLIS from Drexel University in Philadelphia, PA. She is also an active member of several special library associations.

Nicole has been published in several library journals and has also written chapters for *Thinking Outside the Book: Essays for Innovative Librarians* and *Writing and Publishing: The Librarian's Handbook*, both edited by Carol Smallwood. In 2009 she published her first edited work, *Library Mashups: Exploring New Ways To Deliver Library Data*, with Information Today Inc.

You can reach Nicole via email at *nengard@gmail.com*.

About the website

This book comes complete with its very own website. The website will be used to keep readers up to date with open source news, book events and updates to software mentioned within.

More importantly, every link listed in this book will be available on the website. This means that you will not have to type every link you find in the following chapters. Simply visit *http://opensource.web2learning.net* and click the live link there.

Should you find anything you think should be posted to the book's website feel free to email the author at *nengard@gmail.com*.

Acknowledgements

No book is written without the support of many. I'd first like to thank Chris Cormack for introducing me to the world of open source; without him this book would have been written by some other librarian.

I'd also like to thank the entire open source library community; without your contributions and help this book wouldn't be the useful guide that I now think it is. Lastly, I thank my husband, Brian, for his support while I spent endless nights and weekends researching and writing.

Introduction

My introduction to open source software came from one of the original developers of the Koha (*http://koha-community.org*) open source integrated library system, Chris Cormack. It was for this reason that I asked him to write the foreword for this book, so that he could see how much he taught me and share in educating future librarians about the true nature of open source software.

As library budgets worldwide are sliced, librarians look for ways to slim down their spending. It is for this reason that libraries are so interested in learning more about open source software. What they may not realize is that while open source software comes without license fees, and will most likely save them money, open source software is about so much more than a price tag.

As Chris taught me, open source is about openness, sharing, community and collaboration. It is a philosophy as much as a method of software development. As future chapters will elaborate, in the beginning all software was open source; all software was developed in the open and distributed for free among friends and colleagues. The traditional software license that we are used to dealing with in libraries and our homes does not take the form that the first developers envisioned for the future of software.

Knowing this is not enough though. It is my contention that it is essential for libraries to embrace the philosophy behind open source and follow through by participating in open source communities. Over the years I have seen many libraries adopt open source applications, but continue to act as though it were a proprietary system. Using open source software is a rule changer. You no longer need a vendor's approval to add a feature to the system, you no longer have to depend on any one vendor for support, and you no longer get to work in your own library bubble.

What do I mean? Well, as I said, open source software is about community and that means the only way an open source application can survive is if there is an active community behind it. This community can be made up of any combination of developers, software users, bug testers and manual writers.

One misconception that librarians (and many others) have is that to participate in an open source community they must know how to write code; this is not the case. No software application can make it into production if it hasn't first been tested, and who better to test the software than someone who plans to use it daily? No software application is easy to use without well-written documentation, and who better to write that than someone who has learned to use the software the hard way? And no software application without well-organized menus and navigation will be considered user friendly; who better to tell people how to organize things than a librarian?

Librarians have a lot to give to open source software and I hope that after reading this book you will be so excited about what you learned that you will jump in and start to communicate with others who are using and developing open source software to find out how you can participate.

This book is broken into two sections. The first will give you a brief overview of the history and definition of open source software. It includes facts and statistics to combat the fear, uncertainty and doubt (often referred to as FUD) that surround open source and explain why open source software and libraries make the perfect fit. The second section will provide you with a toolbox of open source applications that are being used in libraries right now. Each of these applications will include a first-hand story from a librarian who is using the application regularly. I hope that these insights will help you decide if an application is right for you.

When you are finished with this book you will be able to speak to your colleagues about open source software and make practical suggestions for software improvements in your library. Remember that not every application is right for every library, but you should be able to come away with a few that will either make your workflow more efficient or enable you to provide better services to your patrons.

Part 1
Introduction to open source

What is open source?

The Open Source Initiative defines open source software as software that is distributed with human readable source code in order to allow the user freedom to run, review, alter, enhance and modify the code for any purpose.[1] But open source is about much more than just the code behind the software; it's about community, collaboration and innovation.

In today's world of competing products it might be hard to believe that in the beginning all applications were open source.[2] Donald Rosenberg explained it well when he said that 'open source is not a new way of doing things – it is the original computer way of doing things.'[3] At the same time Eric Raymond reminds us that enthusiasts, artists, tinkerers, problem solvers and experts known as 'hackers' built the internet, World Wide Web, Unix and Linux.[4] Contrary to popular media, to be a hacker is not to be a menace, but to be a computer programmer. This is an important distinction to make early on, since many open source developers proudly call themselves hackers.

Before the internet there was ARPAnet, a transcontinental network only accessible to the US Department of Defense, universities and contractors. This invention brought together hackers from all over the country to collaborate over the network and create applications to make their lives (and eventually all of our lives) easier. It was this connection that brought about the development of many of the world's first open source applications.

The focus of this book is not to go into an in-depth history of open source – for that you can refer any number of amazing titles – but I think it's important at least to talk about some of the hallmarks of open source history to give you a deeper understanding of the ideals around open source and free software.

Scratching an itch

Open source applications often start out with a developer 'scratching an itch' or solving a problem that might be bugging them or their colleagues. Most applications started as a project by one person or a small local group to solve a problem that had been bugging them. Probably the most well known of these projects is the invention of Linux.

It was 1991. Linus Torvalds, a student in Finland, was trying to find an operating system that would work on his PC.[5] When nothing met his needs, he decided to write his own operating system, in effect, scratching his itch. After completing his work (meant only to meet his needs), Linus released his operating system (later to be known as Linux) to his hacker colleagues, to gather comments, suggestions and maybe even get some help improving the product.[6] This project, which started as a hobby, has grown to be the most well-known, most written about and most popular open source project on the web today – and it all started with an itch.[7]

Freedom for all

Linus' free release of Linux to all on the internet has led to a common misconception about open source and free software: that the term 'free' refers to price. In fact, when surveyed in

2009, 36 per cent of library professionals thought that all open source software was free of cost. Although there are open source applications that are free of cost, this is not required by open source and free software licenses. There are more than 60 such licenses, but two account for nearly 90 per cent of all open source software: the GNU General Public License (GPL) and the Berkeley Software Distribution (BSD).

The GPL starts by stating that the term 'free' refers to 'freedom' not price:

> The licenses for most software and other practical works are designed to take away your freedom to share and change the works. By contrast, the GNU General Public License is intended to guarantee your freedom to share and change all versions of a program – to make sure it remains free software for all its users. We, the Free Software Foundation, use the GNU General Public License for most of our software; it applies also to any other work released this way by its authors. You can apply it to your programs, too.
>
> When we speak of free software, we are referring to freedom, not price. Our General Public Licenses are designed to make sure that you have the freedom to distribute copies of free software (and charge for them if you wish), that you receive source code or can get it if you want it, that you can change the software or use pieces of it in new free programs, and that you know you can do these things.[8]

The GPL was written by the Free Software Foundation (*http://fsf.org*). It is important to note here that there are some discrepancies between the definitions of open source software and free software. Despite these differences, for the purposes

1.1 Definition of free software

Free software is a matter of the users' freedom to run, copy, distribute, study, change and improve the software. More precisely, it means that the program's users have the four essential freedoms:

- The freedom to run the program, for any purpose (freedom 0).
- The freedom to study how the program works, and change it to make it do what you wish (freedom 1). Access to the source code is a precondition for this.
- The freedom to redistribute copies so you can help your neighbor (freedom 2).
- The freedom to improve the program, and release your improvements (and modified versions in general) to the public, so that the whole community benefits (freedom 3). Access to the source code is a precondition for this.

Source: Free Software Foundation, Inc., *The Free Software Definition*, 2009, *http://www.gnu.org/philosophy/free-sw.html*.

of this resource, the two will be used interchangeably simply because I agree with Scot Colford when he says that 'for practical purposes they provide the same basic advantages (and challenges) in a library or information science setting.'[9] In fact, this is why many writers will refer to FOSS or F/OSS when talking about free and/or open source software.

While all of the applications discussed later in this book are available for download for free, it is important to realize that there can be monetary costs associated with choosing an open source application.

1.2 Definition of open source software

Introduction

Open source doesn't just mean access to the source code. The distribution terms of open source software must comply with the following criteria:

1. Free Redistribution

The license shall not restrict any party from selling or giving away the software as a component of an aggregate software distribution containing programs from several different sources. The license shall not require a royalty or other fee for such sale.

2. Source Code

The program must include source code, and must allow distribution in source code as well as compiled form. Where some form of a product is not distributed with source code, there must be a well-publicized means of obtaining the source code for no more than a reasonable reproduction cost, preferably downloading via the Internet without charge. The source code must be the preferred form in which a programmer would modify the program. Deliberately obfuscated source code is not allowed. Intermediate forms such as the output of a preprocessor or translator are not allowed.

3. Derived Works

The license must allow modifications and derived works, and must allow them to be distributed under the same terms as the license of the original software.

4. Integrity of The Author's Source Code

The license may restrict source-code from being distributed in modified form *only* if the license allows the distribution of "patch files" with the source code for the purpose of modifying the program at build time. The license must explicitly permit distribution of software built from modified source code. The license may require derived works to carry a different name or version number from the original software.

5. No Discrimination Against Persons or Groups

The license must not discriminate against any person or group of persons.

6. No Discrimination Against Fields of Endeavor

The license must not restrict anyone from making use of the program in a specific field of endeavor. For example, it may not restrict the program from being used in a business, or from being used for genetic research.

Source: Free Software Foundation, Inc., *The Free Software Definition*, 2009, *http://www.gnu.org/philosophy/free-sw.html*.

The costs of open source

Many of us have downloaded and used open source software without ever shelling out a dime. One example for me would be Mozilla's Firefox browser (*http://firefox.com*). I downloaded Firefox for free, installed it in minutes and have never needed to pay for support, development or additional services. Mozilla does give me the opportunity to donate money and/or my time to help with the further development of Firefox. Not all open source applications will be like Firefox.

When looking at open source software it is important to think about the skills within your organization before making a final move. Depending on the people within your organization you may have to outsource some areas of migrating to an open source application. Possible costs that go along with open source might include fees for development or customization, installation, training, help desk or support, and hosting.

Always talk to you staff and see if anyone is using open source applications at home. This may eliminate the need to invest in outside training. For example, when surveyed, 43 per cent of library professionals said they were using OpenOffice (*http://openoffice.org*) at home versus only 29 per cent who were using it at work. That is a large population of your staff who have experience using an application that you may be considering moving to in the near future.

Prevalence of open source

When teaching open source I often ask if anyone in the room is using Firefox and of those who raised their hands how many knew that they were using an open source application. In most cases fewer than half of the attendees knew that they were already using open source software. Tim O'Reilly wrote about a very similar question he asks his audiences:

> I have a simple test that I use in my talks to see if my audience of computer industry professionals is thinking with the old paradigm or the new. 'How many of you use Linux?' I ask. Depending on the venue, 20–80% of the audience might raise its hands. 'How many of you use Google?' Every hand in the room goes up. And the light begins to dawn. Every one of them uses Google's massive complex of 100,000 Linux servers, but they were blinded to the answer by a mindset in which 'the software you use' is defined as the software running on the computer in front of you. Most of the 'killer apps' of the Internet, applications used by hundreds of millions of people, run on Linux or FreeBSD.[10]

The fact is that open source is running more than half of the internet. Netcraft found that Apache ran 52.32 per cent of active websites in January 2010 versus Microsoft, which was running only 17.66 per cent.[11] O'Reilly also notes that there is more open source than just Apache running the internet:

> Much of the role of open source in the development of the Internet is well known: The most widely used TCP/IP protocol implementation was developed as part of Berkeley networking; Bind runs the DNS, without which none of the web sites we depend on would be reachable; sendmail is the heart of the Internet email backbone; Apache is the dominant web server; Perl the dominant language for creating dynamic sites; etc.[12]

While open source software is a new, hot, area of interest for libraries and librarians, open source, as we have seen, is not a new way of doing things.

Sharing

One of the hallmarks of open source is the idea of free collaboration. As stated earlier, open source is not just about the code and the freedom to alter that code. This is why I suggest you talk to your staff and colleagues to see what skills might be hidden in plain view. As librarians we are taught to work collaboratively and it is important to carry that lesson on to our work with open source.

In later chapters I will discuss the idea of sharing and community in open source in more detail.

Notes

1. Free Software Foundation, Inc. 'GNU General Public License version 3 (GPLv3).' *Open Source Initiative*, June 29, 2007. *http://www.opensource.org/licenses/gpl-3.0.html*.
2. Howe, Jeff. *Crowdsourcing: why the power of the crowd is driving the future of business*. New York: Crown Business, 2008. *http://crowdsourcing.typepad.com/*.
3. Rosenberg, Donald K. *Open Source: the unauthorized white papers*. Hungry Minds, 2000.
4. Raymond, Eric S. *The Cathedral and the Bazaar: musings on Linux and open source by an accidental revolutionary*. O'Reilly & Associates, Inc., 2001.
5. Weber, Steve. *The Success of Open Source*. Cambridge, MA: Harvard University Press, 2004.
6. Wayner, Peter. *Free for All: how Linux and the free software movement undercut the high-tech titans*. New York: Harper Business, 2000.
7. Linus writes about his Linux experience in depth in *Just for Fun: the story of an accidental revolutionary*.
8. Free Software Foundation, Inc. 'GNU General Public License version 3 (GPLv3).' *Open Source Initiative*, June 29, 2007. *http://www.opensource.org/licenses/gpl-3.0.html*.
9. Colford, Scot. 'Explaining Free and Open Source Software.' *Bulletin of the American Society for Information Science & Technology* 35, no. 2 (December 2008): 10–14.
10. O'Reilly, Tim. 'Open Source Paradigm Shift.' *O'Reilly Media*, June 2004. *http://www.oreillynet.com/pub/a/oreilly/tim/articles/paradigmshift_0504.html*.
11. 'January 2010 Web Server Survey.' *Netcraft*, January 7, 2010. *http://news.netcraft.com/archives/2010/01/07/january_2010_web_server_survey.html*.
12. O'Reilly, Tim. 'Open Source Paradigm Shift.' *O'Reilly Media*, June 2004. *http://www.oreillynet.com/pub/a/oreilly/tim/articles/paradigmshift_0504.html*.

Community and open source

> The best person to do a job is the one who most wants to do that job; and the best people to evaluate their performance are their friends and peers who, by the way, will enthusiastically pitch in to improve the final product, simply for the sheer pleasure of helping one another and creating something beautiful from which they will all benefit.[1]

Open source is about so much more than the code and the programmers; it's also about the community and the power of the crowd to produce amazing products. Every successful (the key word being 'successful') open source project is backed by a community of developers and application users who keep it alive and kicking. While there are ways to make money from working on open source, you'll find that many of these community members perform their duties to keep learning and share knowledge out of a love for the product and a sense of obligation to the community.[2]

Peter Wayner covers the variety of motives that open source developers have:

> Some contribute source code because it helps them with their day job. Some stay up all night writing code because they're obsessed. Some consider it an act of charity, a kind of noblesse oblige. Some want to fix

bugs that bother them. Some want fame, glory, and the respect of all other computer programmers. There are thousands of reasons why new open source software gets written...[3]

In his chapter on Geek culture, Russell Pavlicek tries to help us understand the motives of open source community. He reminds us that if we are going to understand open source we have to understand the people and the culture behind it.[4]

Working for open source

As professionals, we are all familiar with hierarchy and corporate structure. It is this knowledge that makes it hard to understand how an open source community can develop successful projects without such hierarchy.

Open source communities are self governing and self organizing. This is because there are no executives in charge of deciding the direction of the software for the entire community.[5] The open source community assumes that if enough people need or want a feature it will be written. Remember, open source is about scratching an itch and developers and users alike understand that when the itch arises a development will be submitted for inclusion in the product.

Audris Mockus et al point out that open source software follows a development process that is radically different from the traditional proprietary style of development:

The main differences most often mentioned are the following.

OSS systems are built by potentially large numbers (i.e., hundreds or even thousands) of volunteers. It is worth noting, however, that currently a number of OSS projects are supported by companies and some participants are not volunteers.

Work is not assigned; people undertake the work they choose to undertake.[6]

Working together

To an outsider first joining an existing open source community, these differences in workflow make it look as if there is no control and no rules governing members, but once you become an active member in the community you learn that is not the case. Open source community members follow a series of unwritten rules, no matter what project they are working on.

Rule 1: Communication is key

As most open source projects are worked on by a widespread community, it is key that everyone communicates. Without frequent communication, projects may end up having more than one developer working on implementing a feature instead of working together. It is for this reason that mailing lists associated with active open source projects never sleep. In fact, as Clay Shirky notes, open source communities often have more discussions than would be had among those working on a proprietary programming project.[7]

One key way that open source communities communicate is by sharing ongoing development projects (via bug databases, mailing lists, forums, wikis, and so on) so that everyone knows what is being worked on and time isn't wasted with multiple people working on the same thing.

Rule 2: Honesty is essential (or speak your mind)

If community members cannot be open and honest with each other then things are going to get missed and projects can fail. Pavlicek gets it right:

> In a world where people are constantly exchanging ideas, evaluating concepts, and suggesting enhancements, it is vitally important that everyone speak the truth as he sees it. If someone fails to speak the truth, the process of creating software will be greatly impaired.[8]

This goes hand in hand with communication; if a developer isn't completely honest with the community it can cost the project hundreds of wasted hours in development and planning and, since many open source developers work on these projects in their spare time, this can be devastating.

Rule 3: Respect each other

In any community, there are bound to be disagreements, but it is important to keep in mind that respect is esssential to working together successfully. As is true with most communications, it is important to keep emotion out of messages sent to community members and realize that not everyone thinks the same way that you do. With freedom to develop comes freedom to disagree.

Rule 4: Everyone can be a teacher

In order for open source communities to grow, new members need to be taught the ropes. I speak from personal experience when I say that it can be very scary to jump into a project that has been around and thriving for years. If members of the community aren't willing to teach new people to help out, then there would never be new ideas added to the project and things would become stagnant.

Esther Schindler writes about the importance of mentoring in open source communities (and includes several quotes from Chris and me):

> Some software developers wrinkle their nose at the very idea of deliberate one-on-one help. The default behavior in many (most? it's hard to know) free and open source software (FOSS) communities is to read the code and documentation, try it out, rinse and repeat. People improve their skills on their own; if they need help, they post a note in a forum or ask in IRC [Internet Relay Chat]. Why should it be otherwise?
>
> However, we all learn differently. You might want to settle in with a programming book, while I prefer to take an in-person class. If your project wants to attract new contributors, it behooves you to think past the 'dive into the deep end' culture.[9]

The article goes on to discuss mentoring in several different open source projects with first hand accounts from mentees and mentors.

Rule 5: Keep it transparent

Tying all of the rules together is the simple rule of transparency. Make sure that everything you do and say is out in the open so that everyone can benefit from your opinion, experiences and skills. If you are communicating about the project, log the discussion for those who are not online. If you are writing code, make sure it is submitted to the public repository or logged in a shared database of current projects so that work is not being doubled, and if you teach someone something new, document it and share it with others so they too can learn down the road.

Governing in open source

Even with such utopian rules governing community participation, Steven Weber reminds us that open source is not all about happy, shiny people:

> The open source software process is not a chaotic free-for-all in which everyone has equal power an influence. And it is certainly not an idyllic community of like-minded friends in which consensus reigns and agreement is easy. In fact, conflict is not unusual in this community; it's endemic and inherent to the open source process.[10]

This is why many of these projects have at least one (usually many more) person who is in charge of approving code for inclusion in the project. This person reviews all patches (the common phrase that refers to code updates) as they are submitted and makes sure that they improve the product for the majority of users.

In one of the open source communities that I am active in (the Koha integrated library system; *http://www.koha-community.org*), we have several people on the release team. The person who reviews all patches is known as the release manager (sometimes known as the release coordinator in other communities). Below him is at least one quality assurance person who makes sure that all patches meet the programming guidelines of the community and do not introduce new bugs or security leaks. The release team also has a documentation manager, who is in charge of maintaining and writing documentation for the project; a translation manager, who coordinates with translators all over the world to make sure that the application can be used worldwide; and an interface design manager, who works with the developers to make their interfaces more appealing for those who will be using the software.

Other open source projects are run by foundations or directors of some sort; like everything in open source, there is freedom to choose the type of governance that works best for your product and community. As Weber states, 'There is no off-the-shelf template for coordination and nonauthoritative governance of complexity in the open source setting.'[11]

Whatever roles the community chooses to govern its actions, they never prevent others from chipping in. The whole idea behind open source and the community is that we all help each other in any way possible. So even though my role in the Koha community is as documentation manager, I have been known to test new code and have even written a few patches to fix bugs or add new features, just as others have been known to write documentation.

Health of the community

One of the points I always stress when teaching open source is to make sure that the product you are reviewing has an active and healthy community behind it. As stated earlier, open source is about so much more than working code:

> In considering a FLOSS project, make it a point to understand the community as you familiarize yourself with the code. Subscribe to and skim mailing lists, find

the list archives, and examine the project's Web site. If the project has an Internet relay chat [IRC] channel, spend some time there – IRC's informality can reveal whether participants actually like one another.[12]

Notes

1. Howe, Jeff. *Crowdsourcing: why the power of the crowd is driving the future of business*. New York: Crown Business, 2008. http://crowdsourcing.typepad.com/.
2. Lakhani, Karim R. and Bob Wolf. 'Why Hackers Do What They Do: understanding motivation and effort in free/open source software projects.' In J. Feller, B. Fitzgerald, S. Hissam, and K. R. Lakhani (eds), *Perspectives on Free and Open Source Software*. MIT Press, 2005. *http://opensource.mit.edu/ papers/lakhaniwolf.pdf*.
3. Wayner, Peter. *Free for All: how Linux and the free software movement undercut the high-tech titans*. New York: Harper Business, 2000.
4. Pavlicek, Russell. *Embracing Insanity: open source software development*. Indianapolis, IN: SAMS, 2000.
5. Ibid.
6. Mockus, Audris, Roy Fielding, and James Herbsleb. 'Two Case Studies of Open Source Software Development: Apache and Mozilla.' *ACM Transactions on Software Engineering and Methodology* 11, no. 3 (July 2002): 309–346.
7. Shirky, Clay. *Here Comes Everybody: the power of organizing without organizations*. New York: Penguin Press, 2008.
8. Pavlicek, Russell. *Embracing Insanity: open source software development*. Indianapolis, IN: SAMS, 2000.
9. Schindler, Esther. 'Mentoring in Open Source Communities: what works? what doesn't?' *ITworld*, September 20, 2009. *http://www.itworld.com/open-source/78271/mentoring-open-source-communities-what-works-what-doesnt*.
10. Weber, Steve. *The Success of Open Source*. Cambridge, MA: Harvard University Press, 2004.
11. Ibid.

12. Crowston, Kevin, and James Howison. 'Assessing the Health of Open Source Communities.' *IEEE Computer* 39, no. 5 (2006): 89–91. *http://floss.syr.edu/Presentations/oscon2006/2_Crowston2006Assessing%20the%20health%20of%20open%20source%20communities.pdf.*

Debunking the myths

In my years working in the open source community, I have heard nearly every excuse why people are not using open source. Some of these excuses are specific to libraries and others can be applied to any community worldwide.

Apache runs 52.32 per cent of active websites[1] and Firefox is the web browser of choice for 30.71 per cent of the world's population.[2] So, whether or not librarians realize it, nearly every information organization is using open source software in some way.

Homegrown is not open source

When it came time to automate the card catalog, some libraries decided to try building their own systems. These systems did what the library needed, but staff changes in the library made it clear that homegrown systems were too much trouble. The problem was that libraries built systems that only they knew how to run and update; if libraries had thought to release their code on the internet and work with other libraries, the open source integrated library system would probably be the standard today.

It is this memory that stops many libraries from trying open source applications (particularly open source integrated library systems). It is very important to make it clear that open source software often starts out as homegrown, but has moved on to levels past that. A homegrown system only has those in the home organization to manage and maintain it. A successful open source system has an entire community behind it.

How can it be any good if it's free?

As stated in earlier chapters, people often assume that open source software is free of cost. Many administrators have been known to take this misconception one step further and refuse to use open source for fear that free software surely cannot be as good as other costly options. Assumptions like these are another reason that adoption of open source software in libraries hasn't been as widespread as in other arenas.

So, how do you combat a misconception that is so widespread that we see it in all areas of our lives? We've all heard people, at one time or another, in retail outlets asking why one product is cheaper than another, what's the difference, what is missing from the cheaper product? It's not easy to convince an entire culture that free can be just as good – if not better – than the more pricey alternatives.

The fact, as we've already learned, is that not all open source software is available for free and even if you do receive the software without a monetary payment, there will always be a time contribution necessary to make the switch. That alone won't convince people, of course, but it bears mentioning in order to keep people educated on the topic.

The best way to debunk this particular myth (and others like it) is to provide real world examples and experience. Michael Tiemann points to a study reported in *ACM Transactions on Software Engineering and Methodology* in 2002, which examines the success of big name open source projects, like Apache, Mozilla and Linux:

As empirical data examined so exquisitely by CMU Professor James Herbsleb et al.[3] suggests, a long tail of software developers helps complex systems like Apache and Mozilla achieve functional milestones faster, with fewer defects, which are fixed more rapidly than comparable proprietary software development projects. This empirical evidence supports precisely the same result predicted by game theory models developed by Harvard Business School Professor Carliss Baldwin: free software provides a better architecture *and* a better economic (reward) model for development and innovation than proprietary regimes under a wide range of circumstances. In 2009 these findings were further corroborated when Red Hat was selected to join the S&P 500 index less than 10 years after its IPO. Open Source software development enables a new, viable, and robust model for digital recovery.[4]

Security and open source

Like the concern that free software cannot be as good as expensive software, the common myth that open source software options are not as secure as their proprietary counterparts is not based in fact, but in fear. Studies have shown that despite people's belief that open source software is less secure than proprietary software, open source software is often just as secure and sometimes more secure.

Brian Krebs, who has been writing for *The Washington Post* about technology and computer security since 2000, did an independent study in 2006 that showed that Internet Explorer (IE) was insecure for 284 of 365 days, versus Firefox (the closest open source competitor), which was insecure for only nine days that year:

For a total 284 days in 2006 (or more than nine months out of the year), exploit code for known, unpatched critical flaws in pre-IE7 versions of the browser was publicly available on the Internet. Likewise, there were at least 98 days last year in which no software fixes from Microsoft were available to fix IE flaws that criminals were actively using to steal personal and financial data from users... In contrast, Internet Explorer's closest competitor in terms of market share – Mozilla's Firefox browser – experienced a single period lasting just nine days last year in which exploit code for a serious security hole was posted online before Mozilla shipped a patch to remedy the problem.[5]

It is also important to note here that both Firefox and Internet Explorer are free of cost, but only Firefox is open source.

As mentioned in Chapter 1, Apache, the open source web server, is used by nearly half of all websites.[6] This is not simply because Apache is free of cost; it has to do with the security inherent within the tool, ease of use and of course the features it provides.

Not worth the risk

In addition to the fear that open source software is insecure comes the argument that open source carries with it too many risks. This always make me chuckle a little, because what software doesn't pose some sort of risk these days? We work in a world where computers hold all of our personal information, our memories, our work histories, our financial status and so much more. We trust computers and the software on those computers to keep our lives in order, and when you think about it – that's pretty darn risky!

The question then comes down to what risks are associated with open source software that you are not seeing in the proprietary world? The answer is none. In fact, I'd argue (and others have done the same) that open source actually carries less of a risk that many proprietary options.

One of my favorite quotes regarding the risk of open source comes from Casey Coleman, chief information officer for the US General Services Administration (GSA) in 2008. Coleman says, 'You get much more transparency and interoperability, and that reduces your risk.'[7] She also mentions the fact that by choosing open source the GSA is not tied into contracts with proprietary vendors, giving them all the flexibility that that implies.

In a time when our economy is in flux and companies are being bought out by venture capitalists and other companies, there is no guarantee that the software you are using will be supported next year. By moving to open source you know that you will always be able to use the software, even if the company you were paying for support is bought out or closes its doors. You also have the freedom to hire independent developers to help with customizations and upgrades.

Notes

1. 'January 2010 Web Server Survey.' *Netcraft*, January 7, 2010. *http://news.netcraft.com/archives/2010/01/07/january_2010_web_server_survey.html*.
2. 'Top 5 Browsers from Jan 09 to Feb 10.' StatCounter Global Stats, February 19, 2010. *http://gs.statcounter.com/#browser-ww-monthly-200901-201002-bar*.
3. Mockus, Audris, Roy Fielding, and James Herbsleb. 'Two Case Studies of Open Source Software Development: Apache and Mozilla.' *ACM Transactions on Software Engineering and Methodology* 11, no. 3 (July 2002): 309–346.

4. Tiemann, Michael. 'From Free to Recovery.' *Open Source Initiative*, September 28, 2009. *http://www*.opensource.org/node/471.

5. Krebs, Brian. 'Internet Explorer Unsafe for 284 Days in 2006.' *The Washington Post: Security Fix*, January 4, 2007. *http://blog.washingtonpost.com/securityfix/2007/01/internet_explorer_unsafe_for_2.html*.

6. 'January 2010 Web Server Survey.' *Netcraft*, January 7, 2010. *http://news.netcraft.com/archives/2010/01/07/january_2010_web_server_survey.html*.

7. Quoted in Jackson, Joab. 'GSA Makes the Case for Open Source.' *Government Computer News*, April 16, 2008. *http://gcn.com/blogs/tech-blog/2008/04/gsa-makes-the-case-for-open-source.aspx*.

Open source and libraries

It has been suggested that libraries are almost ethically required to use, develop and support open source software.[1] The parallels between the rules of librarianship and open source are easy to spot just by comparing the open source definition (and/or the free software definition) to the rules set forth by nearly all library associations. Both organizations center their rules on freedom of use and free access to information, a fact that even non-librarians notice:

> Librarians espouse many of the same ideals that drive the free software community. They collaborate and communicate; they work hard to share the results of their work with one another. They understand freedom and feel that it's an important value. That more librarians aren't actively using and evangelizing free software is an indictment against us for not letting them in on our secret.[2]

The Code of Ethics of the American Library Association states, 'We protect each library user's right to privacy and confidentiality with respect to information sought or received and resources consulted, borrowed, acquired or transmitted.'[3] Simply put, members of the American Library Association should deliver information to their patrons without prejudice and without asking what the patron intends to use the information for or with whom they plan to share it. Eric Lease Morgan puts it another way when comparing open source communities to libraries:

> There are many aspects of open source software which are akin to the principles of librarianship. First and foremost in my mind is the expected use of the deliverable – none. In the first case, the deliverable is software. In the second, it is data and information. In both cases, there are very few expectations in regard to what a person does with the information. 'You are free to use and modify the program in any way you desire... It is none of my business why you want to know the answer to this particular reference question or borrow that book.'[4]

This parallel is just one of the reasons why so many libraries have been producing, adopting and promoting open source in recent years. That said, there are still many misconceptions regarding open source software that have slowed library adoption.

Library budgets

One of the most obvious reasons for libraries to consider open source as an alternative to their current systems is shrinking budgets. Open source software usually has either no or low cost to entry and ownership.[5] Because of the nature of the open source license, most open source applications offer a way for software users to demo the product without any limits on time frame or any fees.

Once you have decided to go with an open source product, there is no need to buy licenses for every computer that software will run on, another huge cost saving to libraries. If there are any fees associated with the software it will usually be for support and/or development, both of which libraries can choose to forgo if they feel they have the necessary skills in house to manage the software.

Furthermore, with more and more libraries adopting open source alternatives, the potential for development partnerships becomes more of a reality. A development partnership will allow libraries to pool funds to pay for enhancements to the products, or even to share skilled staff members who will develop the new feature for all libraries in the partnership.

Gift cultures

When the Horowhenua Library Trust (*http://www.library.org.nz*) decided to release their new integrated library system as open source, they gave it the name Koha, the Maori word for gift. This was their gift to the library world, an open source integrated library system for all to benefit from.[6] This is very much in line with gift cultures, which are societies where gifts are made of products and/or services without any explicit request for payment or return services.

Eric Lease Morgan muses about gift cultures, libraries and open source: 'Open source software development and librarianship have a number of similarities – both are examples of gift cultures.'[7] He goes on to explain just how libraries can be considered a gift culture. Most importantly, librarians are known for providing access to information and research without any expectation of monetary exchange. As we all know, most librarians share the information because they love their jobs and furthering the education of others. This is their gift to their communities.

Open source communities follow a very similar model, where community members participate and share their knowledge for the joy of the final product, not a monetary payment. Christina Garsten and Helena Wulff explain this gift giving as the power behind open source software:

> Work, collaboration and sharing of knowledge in open-source communities are culturally organized around the concept of gift giving. Gift giving creates flows of knowledge and makes it possible to innovate and refine software-development processes on a global scale.[8]

This similarity in the ways that libraries and open source both provide gifts to their communities is just another in the long list of reasons why it seems like a logical choice for libraries to use and develop open source software.

Thinking ahead

When I worked at the Jenkins Law Library (*http://www .jenkinslaw.org*) in Philadelphia I did a lot of development to scratch the itches of the library staff. I used an open source language, PHP, and an open source database, MySQL, but I didn't think that anyone else would ever want to use the products I developed and so I didn't think of how to share them with the world. Years later I am an active member in open source library communities and I wish I could go back and think ahead to this moment and the benefits that my tools would have had to other libraries.

While at the law library I developed a powerful content management system to maintain the library's intranet,[9] and now libraries are exploring options like Drupal (*http://www.drupal.org*) and Joomla (*http://www.joomla.org*) to manage their websites. I also wrote an inter-library loan and billing system specific to the law library that I now see would have been useful to integrate into Koha (*http://www.koha-community.org*) or Evergreen (*http://www.open-ils.org*).

I bring this story up because libraries need to think ahead when they start development projects. They need to sit down and say, 'this is what we're going to develop; could it by any chance be of help to other organizations like ours?' It is because of questions like this that we have the amazing selection of library specific open source applications today.

Notes

1. Crawford, Richard. 'Open Source Solutions for Library Needs' presented at the Linux Users Group of Davis, December 5, 2003. *http://www.lugod.org/presentations/oss4lib.pdf*.
2. Eyler, Pat. 'Koha: a gift to libraries from New Zealand.' *Linux Journal* 106 (2003): 1.
3. ALA. 'Code of Ethics of the American Library Association.' American Library Association, January 22, 2008. *http://www.ala.org/ala/aboutala/offices/oif/statementspols/codeofethics/codeethics.cfm*.
4. Morgan, Eric Lease. 'Open Source Software: controlling your computing environment,' March 28, 2009. *http://infomotions.com/musings/oss4cil/index.shtml*.
5. Corrado, Edward M. 'The Importance of Open Access, Open Source, and Open Standards for Libraries.' *Issues in Science and Technology Librarianship* 42 (Spring 2005). *http://istl.org/05-spring/article2.html*.
6. Eyler, Pat. 'Koha: a gift to libraries from New Zealand.' *Linux Journal* 106 (2003): 1.
7. Morgan, Eric Lease. 'Gift Cultures, Librarianship, and Open Source Software Development,' November 14, 2004. *http://infomotions.com/musings/gift-cultures/*.

8. Garsten, Christina, and Helena Wulff. *New Technologies at Work: people, screens, and social virtuality*. Oxford, New York: Berg, 2003.
9. Engard, Nicole C. and RayAna M. Park. 'Intranet 2.0: fostering collaboration.' *Online* 30, no. 3 (2006): 16. *http://www.web2 learning.net/publications-presentations/intranet-20-fostering-collaboration-with-a-homegrown-intranet.*

Part 2
Practical applications
for libraries

Open source for day to day operations

In every business there is a set of operations that must be completed. In today's world, these operations often include the use of a computer. This means that everyone in the workplace must have the same or similar applications on their machines so that they can easily share information back and forth.

Operating system

The one piece of software you need on every computer in your organization is an operating system. When it comes to operating systems, we've all heard of (and probably have some experience with) Microsoft Windows™. Windows is so prevalent in the operating system market that there are some people who think it powers all computers. However, as we've learned in earlier chapters, Windows is not the be all and end all of operating systems; it is just one option available to personal computer users. Other options include a wide variety of Linux (*http://www.linux.org*) flavors.

Due to the open source license associated with the Linux operating system, developers have been able to take the original code and develop several Linux operating systems

5.1 Open source in the real world: Ubuntu

Jessamyn West, Community Moderator at MetaFilter.com
Library Technologist at Tunbridge Library
Tunbridge VT, USA

Why did you decide to use Ubuntu in your library?

We were gifted some computers that were great except for the fact that they had no installed operating system. My choices were to steal a copy of XP [the library had no budget for more software] or get a copy of Ubuntu to work on the two public access PCs. I decided to go with Ubuntu.

How are you using Ubuntu in your library?

Just as public access PC operating systems. We run Firefox and OpenOffice on them mainly but people can access games and a few other programs if they want. People listen to music and surf the web on them mostly; sometimes they word process.

How long have you been using Ubuntu in your library?

This started maybe two to three years ago.

Did you have any trouble implementing Ubuntu in your library?

Not really. I was surprised how easy the implementation was. It's not a very tech savvy community, so switching operating systems on the public wasn't as much of a problem. People just wanted to know 'okay how do I get on the internet?' on these machines; they weren't that cognizant of the operating system. There was still one other PC running Windows that they could use if they have OS-specific tasks to do – chat clients were the biggest problem for people – but they mostly didn't. The install was simple and took a lot less time than any XP install I've done. The two biggest hurdles were getting the librarian to say okay to this idea, and having a safe place for them to put the admin password so that we could find it but that it wasn't available to patrons.

What was the process of switching from proprietary to open source like?

Sort of a no brainer really. Anyone who has dealt with re-installing a corrupt OS knows that it's a serious headache. Being able to wipe/reinstall the OS on this machine or upgrade to the latest version made a lot of the trepidation of public access PCs really go out the window. We could let the public just use the machines how they wanted to and we knew we could fix stuff if it got broken. Just having patrons being able to use a machine that wasn't always popping up dire warnings like 'your computer may be at risk!' was worth the extra effort. With novice computer users, not having their experience be full of fear and uncertainty is a huge deal.

Did you have any help installing, migrating to, or setting up Ubuntu?

No, I read the websites of the support groups and did it myself.

What do you think of Ubuntu now?

I recommend it to people whenever they're complaining about XP or Vista. I think it's basically a shining example of how Linux has become a genuine option for public access computing.

What do others in your library say about Ubuntu?

In some ways they don't even know they're using it. They like that it's free. They like the idea of open source though often they're not that deep into the culture. Libraries have always been about free culture in many ways, this is just another way to forward that ideal.

Anything else you want us to know about Ubuntu or your process of switching to Ubuntu?

I'd rather be someone wrestling with a new operating system than continuing to complain about Microsoft any day.

Learn more

Watch Jessamyn install Ubuntu at *http://vimeo.com/4169783.*

all to serve a difference audience. While any number of these iterations can be used in libraries, I have chosen to focus on Ubuntu (*http://www.ubuntu.com*) because of its ease of use and popularity among librarians and educators.

Why name an operating system Ubuntu? When we look at Windows we understand where the name came from – from all of the windows that you can open and close to view applications and documents. Ubuntu is an African word meaning 'Humanity to others' or 'I am what I am because of who we all are'.[1] In a few of the open source products mentioned throughout this book, you'll find names that embody the open source sentiment, and Ubuntu is one of those.

In my career I have installed several different operating systems – from scratch and as upgrades – and I must say that none was ever as easy as installing Ubuntu. Once installed you have access not only to the operating system but also to several necessary applications like the complete OpenOffice suite, instant messaging software, games, a notepad, and several other necessary applications. If there is an application you are missing you can simply search for it from the built-in directory of Ubuntu-compatible software applications found under the Ubuntu Software Center (see Figure 5.1).

It is for these reasons and of course the $0 price tag that libraries and educational institutions are switching their public machines (and even some staff machines) to Ubuntu.

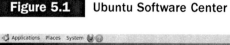

Figure 5.1 Ubuntu Software Center

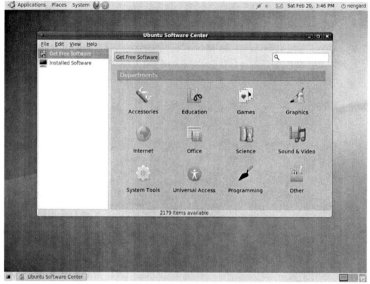

As open source applications go, Ubuntu is one of the better-documented options. You can easily find online and print guides to help with your installation and day to day use of the operating system. The active online community also makes for a great source when needing to find a quick answer.

Virtual machines

As someone who has migrated from one operating system to another I know that it can be very scary to make the switch. This is why I use VirtualBox (*http://www.virtualbox.org*) to test operating systems before making the switch. On my one (and only) computer I have the ability to work in five different operating systems, concurrently or at different times (see Figure 5.2).

Figure 5.2   Four operating systems open in VirtualBox

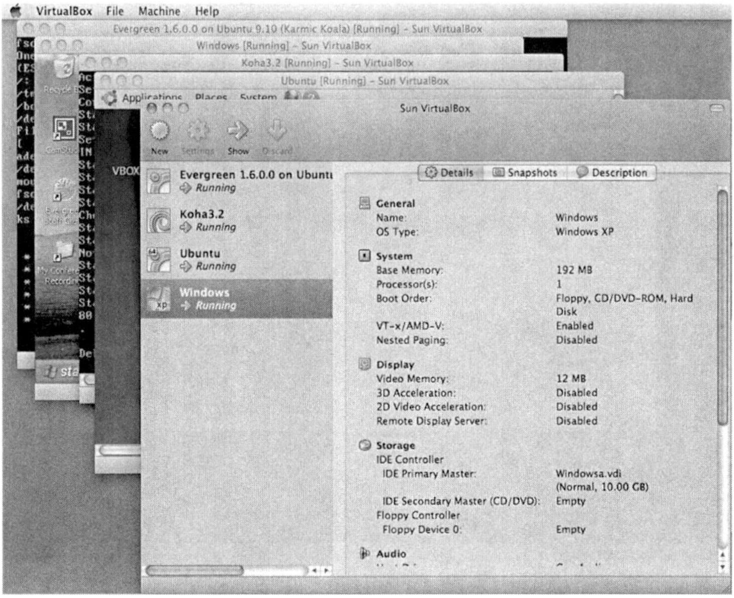

VirtualBox allows you to create multiple virtual machines that make use of your primary machine's hardware while running different software applications. This means that you can install VirtualBox on Windows or Mac OS and then install Ubuntu on it to learn how to use a different operating system before making a blind switch. It also means if you switch to Ubuntu you can still run Windows or Mac OS using VirtualBox.

This would allow libraries that teach technology classes to teach patrons to use multiple operating systems without having multiple operating systems running the machines in the library. As Heather mentions in her summary of VirtualBox, this is not the kind of application that you will use all of the time, but it is a great time and money saver.

5.2 Open source in the real world: VirtualBox

Heather Braum, Technology Librarian
Northeast Kansas Library System
Lawrence KS, USA

Why did you decide to use VirtualBox in your library?

The IT department and many of the staff have Macs, but we still need to be able to have ready access to Windows because most of the libraries we provide technology support to and work with are PC-based. BootCamp would work, except we wanted to use Mac and PCs (and other operating systems) side by side. BootCamp is a one-system solution. You can only run one at a time.

Our network administrator, Liz Rea, needed to be able to run multiple virtual servers in the background on her Mac. Initially, we purchased licenses to the Parallels software, but the program turned out to be clunky, slow and buggy. When launching the software, our computers would freeze for 10 minutes and often would require a reboot. We hated it and other staff members hated it. New versions were available but we didn't want to keep paying for upgrades to the software every time a new version was released, especially when the software never worked well to begin with!

Then we found VirtualBox. We already use a lot of open source software at NEKLS (Koha, WordPress, Firefox and OpenOffice), and so VirtualBox was a natural fit for us. It just works for the times we need it. No freezing or rebooting necessary.

How are you using VirtualBox in your library?

We use it to emulate Windows, Linux flavors and Linux server flavors on Macs. Liz Rea uses it to run a test system of Koha on her iMac so that she can do some testing and figure out the system more.

How long have you been using VirtualBox in your library?

We've been using VirtualBox for about a year now. We don't use it a lot, maybe once or twice a month, but it's quite helpful when we need it.

Did you have any trouble implementing VirtualBox in your library?

No trouble deploying the software itself. Deploying the operating systems within VirtualBox can be easy or difficult. It depends on the version, and how good VirtualBox's drivers are for different operating systems. [Author's note: Both Windows and Ubuntu are supported and easy to install]

What was the process of switching from proprietary to open source like?

The process was easy. No license keys to keep track of or buy (for the emulating software anyway; still needed license keys for the Windows operating systems). VirtualBox ran much faster than Parallels ever did, especially on startup. And, the support on the VirtualBox discussion boards (*http://forums.virtualbox.org*) was great. Usually a question I had had already been asked there.

Did you have any help installing, migrating to, or setting up VirtualBox?

Nope. The only place I consulted was the VirtualBox website and the discussion forums.

What do you think of VirtualBox now?

Love it. I wouldn't want it to be the way I would heavily use Windows, but for the times I quickly need to look at Windows or test out a stripped Windows disk or look at a Linux flavor, it works great. I know it can also be used within Linux and Windows, but I have never used it that way so far.

What do others in your library say about VirtualBox?

Liz Rea, the NEKLS System Administrator, loves it, as well. She's the only other person using it at this time.

Anything else you want us to know about VirtualBox or your process of switching to VirtualBox?

If you're a Mac user and you have that one Windows app you must always use, as long as it's not too system-intensive, check out VirtualBox instead of keeping around a Windows computer just for that one application. Also, if you need to test Linux, but don't have extra hardware lying around, try using VirtualBox to emulate those Linux flavors.

Office suite

Once you have installed your operating system you need an office suite to help with your documenting and calculating needs. Ubuntu comes with the OpenOffice suite (*http://www.openoffice.org*) already installed. If you are not using Ubuntu you can still use OpenOffice because there is a version for every major operating system.

5.3 Open source in the real world: OpenOffice

Kate, Volunteer, Management Collective
Feminist Library
London, UK

Why did you decide to use OpenOffice in your library?

I must admit, this was mostly a financial decision. We are a small, volunteer-run library and a software license for commercial office software wasn't really an option. We discussed an online office suite but our internet access can be a bit temperamental and didn't really want net access to be a prerequisite for access. We toyed with the idea of installing Linux on some of the older PCs in the office, but weren't ready for that step just yet. Using a cross-platform suite leaves that option open for later.

How are you using OpenOffice in your library?

We use OpenOffice for most administrative work conducted in the Feminist Library. Recently, as we have moved our catalogue to a library management system and are in the midst of a big cataloguing project, we have been creating an index of some parts of the collection and using CALC spreadsheets to convert data into MARC records to import to the new catalogue.

How long have you been using OpenOffice in your library?

Basically, since we've revived the library in mid 2008. I'm not sure whether it was used in previous incarnations of the library before I became involved.

Did you have any trouble implementing OpenOffice in your library?

Some slight glitches with file formats when sharing documents with other organizations but the interface for OpenOffice is very user friendly and our formatting needs aren't particularly complex. So, while not all the volunteers are as geeky as others, there have been precious few troubles with implementation and everyone adjusted easily.

As we rely on the work of volunteers, we need to be able to access our work at the library as well as at home or in the office, so the only adjustments needed were in terms of compatibility across a variation of environments. Luckily, we started with OpenOffice 3 so compatibility wasn't as much of an issue as it could have been.

What was the process of switching from proprietary to open source like?

The transition to OpenOffice was pretty straightforward as the basics of word processing and other productivity software are quite similar. Plus, some of us were already using it at home or in other projects, which helped make the transition even easier. OpenOffice has also proved to be a stepping stone to other F/OSS and I now feel our move towards open source is an ethical as well as a financial choice for us.

Did you have any help installing, migrating to, or setting up OpenOffice?

My role at the library is mostly as a volunteer systems librarian, so I look after the software installation, set up and maintenance. The only concern in migrating to OpenOffice was about accessing older documents in proprietary file formats but even that didn't prove much of a problem.

What do you think of OpenOffice now?

I still think it's great and don't see a reason to go back to proprietary software. The way we work depends so much on portability and a non-centralized approach (for want of a better description) that we can't really rely on being able to access our files only on one type of computer, in one set of circumstances. And, as I mentioned before, I think OpenOffice is a great first step in the world of F/OSS.

What do others in your library say about OpenOffice?

Everyone in the management collective is happy using OpenOffice and more and more of us use it at home now too, so it wasn't such a big shift. It takes a bit of time to adjust to a slightly different interface but hasn't proved a problem. Volunteers at the library have varying degrees of interest and experience in the systems side of things, but using free and open source systems has helped increase interest, if only a little bit.

OpenOffice is a complete office suite with word processing, spreadsheets, databases, image editing and presentations, all of which have menus that are very similar to other office suites (see Figure 5.3); this has the advantage of making the transition easy. With over 20 years of development behind it,[2] OpenOffice is extremely stable and full of great features.

Like Ubuntu this is an application that many libraries are putting on their public stations to allow community members access to powerful applications without having to pay the license fees for each computer. It is also very easy to bring information from other office suites into OpenOffice because it can read in and write out to several different formats – one of my favorite features in OpenOffice is the ability to save a document as a PDF.

Figure 5.3   Word processing in OpenOffice

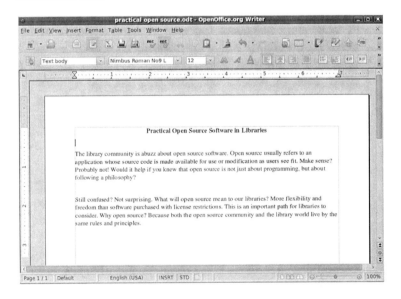

Statistics and data gathering

Many libraries find it useful to keep statistics of their day-to-day operations. In some libraries this is done with a piece of paper and a pen, others use a simple spreadsheet, and some use the open source Libstats (*http://code.google .com/p/libstats/*) application.

5.4 Open source in the real world: Libstats

Kelly M. Broughton, Assistant Dean, Research and Education Services
Ohio University Libraries
Athens OH, USA

Why did you decide to use Libstats in your library?

We chose Libstats to facilitate and ease the effort of data collection, as well as work on standardization across a variety of service points.

How are you using Libstats in your library?

We use Libstats to track reference, technical and directional questions in the libraries (how many, how long, from which service point and via what communication method – in person, email, phone, IM and so on).

How long have you been using Libstats in your library?

We began piloting in May 2009 and implemented it fully in summer 2009.

Did you have any trouble implementing Libstats in your library?

None that our techs couldn't overcome.

Did you have any help installing, migrating to, or setting up Libstats?

Library IT and reference staff worked together on implementation and customization.

What do you think of Libstats now?

Nothing but good things.

What do others in your library say about Libstats?

Really easy! Desk students like it better than the hash marks we used to use.

Libstats is a very simple application (see Figure 5.4) developed solely to help librarians keep statistics on reference queries and a knowledge base of frequently answered questions. Using the data stored in the Libstats database librarians can easily generate reports on the numbers of questions, where questions arrive from (email, phone, walk-in), and what types of questions are asked (general reference, database related, and so on).

Another way to collect data is to survey your patron base. There are many popular web applications that can be used for this task, but there are limitations and costs associated

Figure 5.4 Adding a question to the knowledge base in Libstats

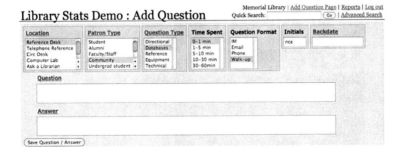

5.5 Open source in the real world: LimeSurvey

Vincci Kwong, Head of Web Services
Franklin D. Schurz Library, Indiana University South Bend
South Bend IN, USA

Why did you decide to use LimeSurvey in your library?

Cost, features and flexibility.

How are you using LimeSurvey in your library?

Currently, we use LimeSurvey to collect institutional research information from students who take the Introduction to Information Literacy (Q110) class. The survey basically asks if students would give permission for us to use their pre-test and post-test results for research purposes. We are also planning to set up the pre-test and post-test of Q110 using LimeSurvey as data can be exported to different formats; it makes it easy to perform data analysis.

How long have you been using LimeSurvey in your library?

More than a year; we started to use LimeSurvey in August 2008.

Did you have any trouble implementing LimeSurvey in your library?

Before the installation, I found out that our server didn't meet the system requirements for LimeSurvey, as mbstring was not installed as part of PHP; however, we did get the issue resolved. Another problem we encountered was related to exporting data. We were able to export data to .csv format, but VVExport didn't work for us. This issue was finally resolved by an upgrade of the software.

Did you have any help installing, migrating to, or setting up LimeSurvey?

We got help from our campus IT department and the LimeSurvey forums when we installed the software.

What do you think of LimeSurvey now?

We like LimeSurvey, but it would be better if the user interface for creating surveys were more intuitive and self-explanatory.

What do others in your library say about LimeSurvey?

The librarian who uses LimeSurvey regularly told me that it was easy to use.

with them. When I started writing this book, I went out on a hunt for open source survey applications and came across LimeSurvey (*http://limesurvey.org*).

LimeSurvey (see Figure 5.5) is an open source application that resides on your local web server. This means that you can host as many polls and surveys as you want without incurring any extra fees. Since LimeSurvey is such a powerful

Figure 5.5   Sample LimeSurvey results display

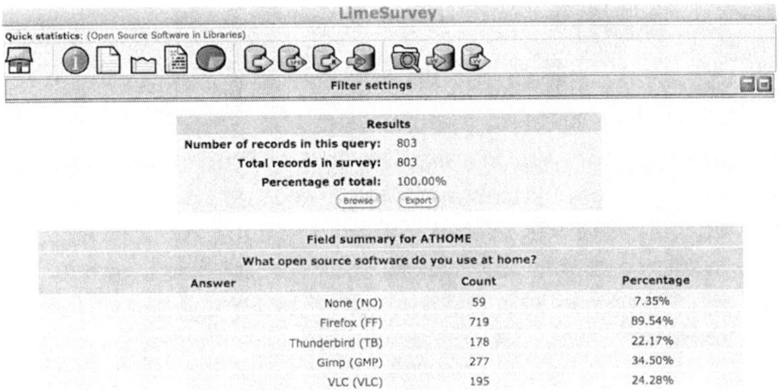

tool, it does take a bit of learning to figure out how to best create a survey for your library, but the documentation for the product is outstanding and very easy to follow.

Using LimeSurvey you can set up surveys to ask your patrons what they think about the library, what they want to see from the library, or just what their favorite types of books or movies are. It also offers you the ability to create polls in multiple languages, allowing you to reach a wider audience. As the application is run from your own server, you can control the look of the surveys as well as the time the survey remains available for answering.

Improving day to day services

The applications in this chapter are all meant either to replace applications you may be spending too much time and money on or to provide your library with a service that you maybe didn't think you could afford before. Libraries worldwide are making the switch to open source for applications such as these, to provide patrons with improved services and the staff with functionalities they would not be able to afford otherwise.

Notes

1. 'What is Ubuntu?' Ubuntu, 2010. *http://www.ubuntu.com/products/whatisubuntu*.
2. 'Why OpenOffice.org.' *OpenOffice.org*, 2009. *http://why.openoffice.org/*.

6

Open source web access

There isn't a day that goes by when librarians do not have to access the internet in one way or another. We have research to do online, reference questions to answer via email and books to buy from our vendors online, and just as our computers do not need to use proprietary software, so too is proprietary software unnecessary for us to access the web.

Open source web browsing

If you were to make the switch to only one open source application in this book (and I hope that is not the case), Firefox (*http://www.firefox.com*) is for you (see Figure 6.1). Firefox has taken the web browser from being a way to read web pages to being a way to interact fully with the web. The power of Firefox lies in its open source architecture; because anyone can see how Firefox works behind the scenes, they can easily expand on it by writing add-ons and suggesting overall code improvements.

As with most open source applications, Firefox is also known for being able to address bugs and security leaks quickly by releasing minor updates in between release cycles. One of the greatest, and most misguided, concerns library administrators have about switching to Firefox is security.

A study done in 2006 by Brian Krebs of Security Fix (*http://voices.washingtonpost.com/securityfix/*) showed that for at least 98 days of 2006 'no software fixes from Microsoft were available to fix [Internet Explorer] flaws that criminals were actively using to steal personal and financial data from users.'[1] In contrast, there was a single period of only nine days that year when Firefox was left without a patch to a serious security hole.

With data like this it becomes hard to believe that Firefox is less secure than Internet Explorer. As part of its default framework, Firefox includes security functionality such as pop-up blocking, anti-malware, anti-phishing, parental controls and private browsing. If that's not enough, you can extend Firefox to include even more protection for yourself and your patrons.

6.1 Open source in the real world: Firefox

Greg Johnson, Digital Initiatives and Systems Librarian
Governors State University
University Park IL, USA

Why did you decide to use Firefox in your library?

We had too many problems with Internet Explorer crashing. Plus students seem to like it better.

How are you using Firefox in your library?

We have made Firefox the default internet application for use on all of the library computers.

How long have you been using Firefox in your library?

About one year.

Did you have any trouble implementing Firefox in your library?

It took a little while for students to stop looking for the ubiquitous Internet Explorer icon, but after that, we have not had any problems.

What was the process of switching from proprietary to open source like?

Easy.

Did you have any help installing, migrating to, or setting up Firefox?

Since it comes from out of the download fully loaded and ready to go, all we needed to do was set the main library page as the home page and image it out to all the computers.

What do you think of Firefox now?

It is one of the best browsers available for personal computers.

What do others in your library say about Firefox?

Oddly enough, librarians are not fans of Firefox. Other technical staff members prefer to use either Firefox or Google Chrome, both open source options.

In addition to the efficient development process and built in security, Firefox also offers many useful add-ons to increase privacy, security and overall efficiency. These are just a few of the reasons why libraries have been switching their public stations (if not all of the computers in the library) to use Firefox as the default browser.

Of the thousands of available add-ons, my favorite is AdBlockPlus (*http://adblockplus.org*). AdBlockPlus blocks nearly every ad on the web from loading in your browser. Another way to protect yourself is by preventing scripts from running without asking you first. One add-on that many librarians use is FlashBlock (*https://addons.mozilla.org/ en-US/firefox/addon/433*), which prevents all Flash scripts from running in your browser without you first clicking a

Figure 6.1 Firefox browser

'play' button. Another add-on that prevents scripts from running is NoScript (*https://addons.mozilla.org/en-US/firefox/addon/722*). Once installed, NoScript prevents executable content from running without your express permission.

To find more security add-ons for Firefox you can browse through its security add-ons section (*https://addons.mozilla.org/en-US/firefox/browse/type:1/cat:12*).

Expanding Firefox

I mentioned earlier that Firefox has grown to be so much more than a web browser; it can also work to assist you with your research. One popular tool among libraries is LibX (*http://libx.org*).

LibX is an open source browser toolbar that you can customize to help patrons (and staff for that matter) find library resources while browsing. Once the LibX toolbar is installed it puts a search box for the library catalog at the top of the user's browser (no need to visit the library catalog website).

6.2 Open source in the real world: LibX

Chris Keene, Technical Development Manager
University of Sussex Library
Brighton, East Sussex, UK

Why did you decide to use LibX in your library?

Looked interesting and decided to set it up when I had a free hour or so.

How are you using LibX in your library?

We have a public LibX toolbar which is not very well promoted. It can search our local catalogue (we use two, Aquabrowser and Talis Prism), online journals and link resolver, and allows people off campus to reload a page using EZproxy. It also searches the local public library catalogue, which we've had some good feedback on.

In addition we have a staff toolbar; this was in part to streamline our reading list processes. Staff can right click on a book title or ISBN and search our catalogue and, more importantly, Coutts Oasis (a book supplier online ordering system, which links in to our library management system – via EDI Quotes – and creates orders). We use OCLC's xISBN a lot so that staff can right click on an ISBN and find out if we have that book in stock regardless of edition and so on. We are currently trying to integrate xISBN and Coutts Oasis.

How long have you been using LibX in your library?

We have had a public toolbar for a couple of years but have only recently started to use it.

Did you have any trouble implementing LibX in your library?

The configuration website is very good, but does have some quirks. Getting it to do exactly what we want it to do has been slow at times.

We have had no real non-technical problems. I think we would have done if we heavily promoted it, especially on the main library catalog. There would have been questions as to how we support it, how we manage changes, about training and worry that it would confuse users with low IT levels. By promoting it on 'tech-friendly' channels (such as Twitter) and keeping it low key we have avoided this.

What was the process of switching from proprietary to open source like?

I would say it wasn't a switch. It wasn't a key need, which one product catered for and then it was replaced with LibX. I came across it, spent a few hours setting it up, showed a couple of people and quietly made it public, refining it since then.

We already use open source applications (EPrints) and infrastructure (Apache, Linux and so on) and would certainly use it again for other needs (for example OPACs such as VuFind).

Did you have any help installing, migrating to, or setting up LibX?

No, but the help on the website was good. And I come from a computer science background.

What do you think of LibX now?

Fantastic and very useful. I think the context menu options are more useful than the toolbar (already have too many toolbars!) and I would like to see it developed further.

> I do wish it provided usage statistics per library, on the number of downloads and so on.
>
> **What do others in your library say about LibX?**
>
> The staff love it, especially those in our resources departments (reading lists, acquisitions, cataloguing) who are always under pressure to improve their efficiency. It has proved a time saver. Users seem to like it too, though we have had little feedback.

LibX also has several scripts that integrate the library into popular websites like Amazon.com (*http://amazon.com*), Google Scholar (*http://scholar.google.com*) and Barnes & Noble Online (*http://bn.com*). When you search on any of these, links back to the library appear on your results. For Amazon and Barnes & Noble, links will take you into a library catalog search for the book in question. When on Google Scholar, each article is followed by a link to the library databases to search for the article, a nice little reminder that not everything is available for free online (see Figure 6.2).

Over 700 libraries have set up LibX toolbars and many more are added daily, simply because the tool used to create a toolbar specifically for your library is so easy to use. First, you want to be sure that you have all of the necessary proxy information for your databases and catalog. Next, enter the LibX builder and start answering questions. You will be asked for information about connecting to your library catalog and subscription databases. You will also be prompted to brand your LibX toolbar by adding an icon or logo for your library.

Figure 6.2 The LibX VT toolbar

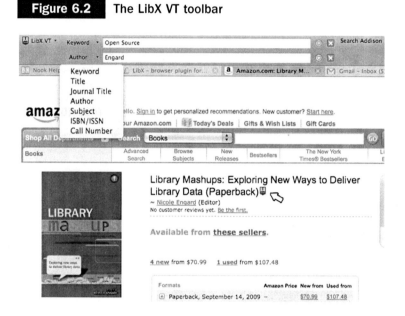

Once your toolbar is done you will want to install it on every computer in the library and promote it heavily on your library website so that your patrons download and use it at home.

Another favorite open source tool that integrates into Firefox is Zotero (*http://zotero.org*), which is a citation management tool that allows you to save references to your computer for easy access and bibliography creation.

Once Zotero is installed, it is possible to save citations from many popular research sites and databases[2] with one click, through a button which appears in your status bar. Once in Zotero you can organize your resources using folders, tags and notes. You can also export resources directly to many word processing applications, including OpenOffice, in the citation format of your choosing. Zotero allows you to store all of your research materials in various folders right in your browser (see Figure 6.3).

Figure 6.3 A search for 'Koha' on Zotero

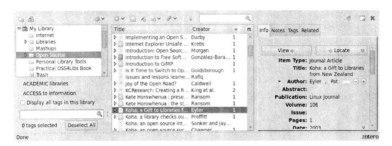

Zotero also has the ability to share your resources over a network with other Zotero users, making group projects and librarian research projects much easier for everyone involved. With an account on Zotero.org you can sync the resources you save on your computer with your collection on the web. This works as a backup and a way to share your resources with your colleagues or fellow researchers.[3]

6.3 Open source in the real world: Zotero

Jason Puckett, Instruction Librarian for User Education Technologies, and Journalism and Speech Liaison
Georgia State University Library
Atlanta GA, USA

Why did you decide to use Zotero in your library?

I had been teaching EndNote for several years when I discovered Zotero. I didn't really start using it until I installed Linux on my laptop at home, which of course can run Zotero but not EndNote. I was blown away by how much easier it was to use and how easy it was to incorporate into the research process. I dropped EndNote immediately and put together a web guide and a workshop plan. I was the first person to start promoting it at the GSU Library, and I've been very gratified to see interest skyrocket since I got here last year.

I'm a fan of the benefits of open source software in general, and all other things being equal I prefer to use it when I can, but realistically some OSS products just aren't as slick and easy to use as their commercial equivalents. That's not the case with Zotero. It's much easier to use than any other citation manager I've tried, and the latest version is a lot more versatile and powerful than EndNote. I like the fact that it's designed by academic researchers for academic researchers, since the developers really seem to understand how people are using it.

It's also a lot easier to install, which sounds like a small thing but is a big headache for those of us providing EndNote support at GSU. We have a site license for EndNote, so we have it available to download, but users have to log in, download a huge installation file, and in order to end up with a full authenticated installation they have to follow some specific steps during the install process. Despite providing instructions and a tutorial video, that's still the number one problem our users have with EndNote. No such difficulty with Zotero.

How are you using Zotero in your library?

I've got a web guide that gets a lot of traffic. I've been teaching regular drop-in workshops in the library. I do a lot of one-on-one help for students and faculty. I've given presentations to some departments on campus. I'm starting some online workshops in a couple of weeks, which I've done for EndNote in the past and I think will work well for Zotero.

How long have you been using Zotero in your library?

I've been in my present job for about a year. I'd guess I was using it for two or three years before that at my previous library, so three to four years total.

Did you have any trouble implementing Zotero in your library?

Only a couple of minor hitches. One is having both EndNote and Zotero installed on our computers, since one program may want to grab downloaded citations away from the other, but it's easy enough to disable Zotero temporarily if that's a problem. (That can take a little time on every computer in a large classroom, though.)

The other is that it only works with Firefox, but I've even talked a few people into switching to Firefox solely so they could use Zotero.

What was the process of switching from proprietary to open source like?

I can't say that we've entirely switched, nor are we likely to stop supporting EndNote as far as I can see. A lot of the campus still uses EndNote, but the two programs are coexisting happily so far. It helps that you can easily export data from one program to the other, and I do like having both options available to our users.

Did you have any help installing, migrating to, or setting up Zotero?

I asked my IT department to install it on the public computers and in our classrooms. They were great about setting it up, though they asked not to put on the latest version since it's still in beta. That worked fine for me. They had no questions or concerns about using an open-source product. I think it's easier for them since they don't have to track licenses and so forth.

What do you think of Zotero now?

I love it. I'd marry it if our society weren't so closed-minded. I use it constantly, for research, work projects, and keeping personal reading lists. The community of users and developers is incredibly helpful and creative. My friend Kathryn Greenhill just posted a great video about using it to collect image credits for presentations, which I'd never thought of even though I knew it works great with Flickr. I share citations with friends and colleagues online. And I love that it keeps my citation library up to date effortlessly on computers with different operating systems, and updates itself automatically.

What do others in your library say about Zotero?

I'm finding that it's very easy to pick up and use for students who haven't used a bibliographic manager before. An English professor has asked me to teach it to her freshman class next week as part of their research assignment, which I think is great since most students don't get exposed to citation managers until much later.

I once had a student make an appointment with me for an EndNote consultation. I spent 45 minutes showing her how EndNote works, and then I mentioned Zotero as an alternative and showed it to her in five. She said 'I wish I'd known about Zotero to begin with. I'm using that instead.'

A colleague stopped by my desk one morning and said a student was having trouble doing something in EndNote, so he just recommended they switch to Zotero and they went away happy. I've also been asked why the university still pays for an EndNote license.

Anything else you want us to know about Zotero or your process of switching to Zotero?

Once, after I got back from a vacation in England, a friend asked if it was hard to readjust to driving on the right side of the road again. I said no, it was sort of like being allowed to relax and stop juggling. That's what the experience of switching from EndNote to Zotero was like for me.

Learn more

Check out Jason's guide to Zotero (*http://research.library.gsu.edu/zotero*).

A new browsing experience

This chapter has only scratched the surface of the amazing tools available to enhance Firefox and improve users' browsing experience. There are entire books on the market that can tell you more, or you can simply visit the Firefox website and start browsing through the add-ons database to see what is available.

Open source emailing

At library and technology conferences worldwide I always hear that email is dead, but I respectfully disagree, as would many librarians. Email is central to our communication workflow and so we need a tool that is up to the task. Mozilla's Thunderbird (*http://www.mozillamessaging.com/ thunderbird*) is that very tool.

6.4 Open source in the real world: Thunderbird

Kyle M. Hall, IT Technician
Crawford County Federated Library System
Crawford County PA, USA

Why did you decide to develop Thunderbird for your library?

We decided to switch to Thunderbird as our primary email client because it had become the most popular OSS solution at the time. Previously, we had used Mozilla as both a web browser and email client, but when we switched to Mozilla Firefox as our primary web browser, we needed a new email client; the obvious choice was Mozilla's new email client, Thunderbird.

How are you using Thunderbird in your library?

Nearly all our librarian's desktop computers have Thunderbird installed to access their email from our mail server via SMTP.

How long have you been using Thunderbird in your library?

We have been using Thunderbird since late 2003.

Did you have any trouble implementing Thunderbird in your library?

The only issues we've had were the initial configuration issues. We use TLS for security, and sometimes Thunderbird would refuse to connect to our mail server properly. Thankfully, those issues seem to have been resolved with the newer version of the program.

What was the process of switching from proprietary to open source like?

We had previously used Netscape, then Mozilla as our email clients, so the switch was relatively painless. The process involved only configuring the client, as well as importing the contact list from our previous client.

Did you have any help installing, migrating to, or setting up Thunderbird?

No, we did all the work in-house.

What do you think of Thunderbird now?

I think Thunderbird is a great program, but the advent of good web-based e-mail has made it much less essential than it used to be. Our mail server currently runs on Zimbra, so our librarians have the choice of using Thunderbird or a web-based interface to check their email. Most librarians still choose to use Thunderbird.

What do others in your library say about Thunderbird?

Our librarians are simply happy to use an email client that works consistently and correctly nearly all the time.

Anything else you want us to know about Thunderbird or your process of switching to Thunderbird?

Using SMTP instead of POP3 as your standard email protocol makes switching between clients much easier, as there is no need to export and import the email messages themselves.

Many librarians are used to email clients like Microsoft Outlook or Novell Groupwise and the idea of changing from a familiar interface to an unknown can be scary. However, Thunderbird's design is very similar to other email tools, offering several panels for viewing your messages, your contacts, your tasks and more (see Figure 6.4).

Thunderbird even allows for personal and shared calendars with the use of the Lightning add-on (*http://www .mozilla.org/projects/calendar/lightning/*). Lightening allows

Figure 6.4 Thunderbird screen showing several panels for viewing messages, contacts, tasks and more

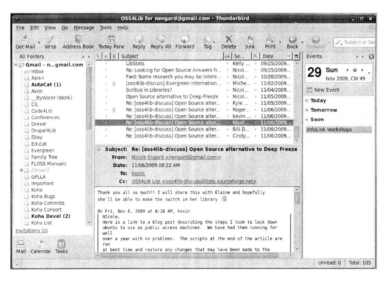

you to create calendars on your local machine or access shared calendars through the network, which is an important feature for anyone working in an office (see Figure 6.5).

If your library uses Google Apps for email and calendaring needs, you can still use Thunderbird by installing the Provider for Google Calendar add-on (*https://addons.mozilla.org/en-US/thunderbird/addon/4631*) and the Gmail IMAP Account Setup add-on (*https://addons .mozilla.org/en-US/thunderbird/addon/6381*). These tools grab your content directly from Google and publish it to Thunderbird dynamically.

In addition to a simple interface, Thunderbird has built-in spam filters, the option to download other security add-ons (*https://addons.mozilla.org/en-US/thunderbird/browse/ type:1/cat:66*), powerful mail searching functionality and the ability to check multiple email accounts at once (including popular web-based email accounts like Gmail and Yahoo! Mail).

Figure 6.5 Lightening, showing a calendar integrated within Thunderbird

Instant messaging

While we can all agree that email is not dead, this does not mean that it is our sole means of communication online. Many libraries have started to offer instant messaging reference services as an additional way to allow patrons to reach them. Pidgin (*http://www.pidgin.im*) is an open source instant messaging tool that can make communicating with your patrons much simpler. Pidgin makes it easy to connect to several IM clients at once and keep your contacts organized for quick communication.

Pidgin allows you to log into all of the popular instant messaging clients – AIM, Yahoo!, GTalk, Windows Live

Figure 6.6	Pidgin screen showing connections to several IM clients

Messenger, and more – at one time. Like many other open source applications, Pidgin also has plugins (*http://developer .pidgin.im/wiki/ThirdPartyPlugins*) available that will add access to additional instant messaging networks like Facebook and Twitter. This single interface allows librarians to monitor several communication channels at once without having to install and run multiple applications (see Figure 6.6).

6.5 Open source in the real world: Pidgin

Jennifer M. Turner, Support and Training Specialist
PALS, A Program of the Minnesota State Colleges and Universities
Mankato MN, USA

Why did you decide to use Pidgin in your library?

Pidgin works with a variety of different IM programs, connects to professional IRC channels, and keeps a log of conversations/discussions. Also, it's free and easy to use!

How are you using Pidgin in your library?

Communication with colleagues – we provide technical support and training for the library system used by a majority of Minnesota's colleges and it is often easier to send coworkers a link to a problem rather than have them try to recreate the issue on their end. It has also come in handy when a person is working from a remote location and has an issue or question for another staff person.

How long have you been using Pidgin in your library?

About six months (very approximate guess).

Did you have any trouble implementing Pidgin in your library?

No problems with the actual software, but few staff members have adopted its use. Those of us that do use it are pleased.

> **Did you have any help installing, migrating to, or setting up Pidgin?**
>
> None.
>
> **What do you think of Pidgin now?**
>
> It's great! And the more I learn about it, the more I like it!
>
> **What do others in your library say about Pidgin?**
>
> Those who use it have embraced it and use it for both professional and personal communication. Those who don't use it don't say much about it, as they are unfamiliar with it (and don't really use chat services in general)

A web of options

I have briefly discussed open source options available to your library. There are many more open source applications available to make your online experiences more efficient and more secure. Give the applications in this chapter a chance and if you find you aren't pleased, search for other open source alternatives; there are plenty out there.

Notes

1. Krebs, Brian. 'Internet Explorer Unsafe for 284 Days in 2006.' *The Washington Post: Security Fix*, January 4, 2007. *http://blog.washingtonpost.com/securityfix/2007/01/internet_ explorer_unsafe_for_2.html*.
2. To find a full list of sites that support Zotero you can check their list of compatible sites (*http://www.zotero.org/translators*). You can also find out what library software supports Zotero on their list of compatible software (*http://www.zotero.org/ support/compatible_standards_and_software*).
3. My public Zotero library can be found at *http://www.zotero.org/ nengard*.

Open source media applications

Many academic libraries offer their students access to a media center in the library. A common misconception is that smaller libraries do not have the budget to offer such services to their patrons, but there are plenty of open source applications that can be used to populate a media center in any library.

Photo editing

When it comes to photo editing and creation, many libraries stick to using the clip art package that came with their word processing application because they think that is all that they can afford. In reality there are many powerful open source tools available to make your photos look more professional. The first and probably the best known of these tools is GIMP (*http://gimp.org*).

GIMP is a photo editing suite that has been compared to Adobe® Photoshop®. Photoshop® is meant for the professional artist, and can often be overkill for the average library. GIMP offers libraries an affordable alternative. According to the official GIMP website:

7.1 Open source in the real world: GIMP

Chauncey G. Montgomery, Director
Community Library
Sunbury OH, USA

Why did you decide to use GIMP in your library?

Staff and customers were in need of a graphics manipulation program and products like Adobe Photoshop® were too costly for a small library with limited funds. From what we saw, GNU Image Manipulation Program (GIMP) provided a full range of features, similar to Photoshop®, and looked intuitive enough to implement in the library.

How are you using GIMP in your library?

Customers use GIMP to do light photo editing. The images they edit tend to be uploaded to photo sites, or sent to local photo labs for printing.

Library personnel use GIMP for more advance image manipulation. Images for the web, displays, posters, bookmarks and various promotional materials are often first edited using GIMP. It has primarily become the image manipulation tool for the library.

Some of the common uses of GIMP in the library include but are not limited to cropping, resizing and adjusting levels. We also use the layers feature when adjusting or building more complex images.

A sample of an image we built using GIMP can be seen in Figure 7.6. This image is used for the header for a local history photo journal at the library. Figure 7.6 shows an image created in GIMP that is used for the header for a local history photo journal at the library.

How long have you been using GIMP in your library?

We have been using GIMP for probably three years now.

Did you have any trouble implementing GIMP in your library?

We had no problems implementing GIMP with customers because prior to GIMP, the public had no access to an image manipulation program. Often times we do need to assist customers with editing because they are not familiar with the tools in GIMP and how to properly use them.

For most staff, we've had the same response as we did with the public. Prior to GIMP, most staff did not have access to a manipulation application. They have been successful in carrying out simple tasks with the program.

We have one individual who is using an older version of Photoshop® Elements and is reluctant to use GIMP. On the other hand, I have been forced to use GIMP for all editing needs at the library as I am using a Linux workstation and it is the only tool I have available.

I often use Photoshop® for personal use and using GIMP has left me with two impressions in relation to Photoshop®. First, I am impressed with the power and functionality of GIMP. Almost anything I do in Photoshop® can be done in GIMP. With that said, my second impression is that GIMP is not as intuitive as Photoshop®. Likewise, it is somewhat cumbersome with the three separate windows, as opposed to the single interface for Photoshop®. Overall, though, I think it is easy enough that someone can sit down and do simple image manipulation without much training or study.

What was the process of switching from proprietary to open source like?

It has been much easier than I had imagined several years ago when we started moving in this direction. I am extremely impressed with the availability of quality, powerful software. Any time I have need for an application, I can usually find an open source solution. Installation is always just as easy as proprietary, and use, for the most part, is just as intuitive.

Open source has plenty of support. You just have to be a little more patient. Most likely the application can do what you want it to do, but you need to spend time searching forums, sending emails, or just playing with the application to discover how you complete the desired task.

Did you have any help installing, migrating to, or setting up GIMP?

We did not have any help installing and migrating to GIMP; however, it is extremely easy to install.

What do you think of GIMP now?

I think that it is just as good as Photoshop® Elements and someone who has never used Elements or the full version of Photoshop® would have no trouble getting into GIMP and using it.

What do others in your library say about GIMP?

Most feel that it does the job. The individual on staff who uses Photoshop® Elements is probably a little more apprehensive to embrace GIMP but doesn't say anything bad about it; she just doesn't use it (probably because she has an option).

Anything else you want us to know about GIMP or your process of switching to GIMP?

Just install it and start using it. You should have no problems whatsoever. Be patient if you can't figure out how to do something. Read websites, forums and, if need be, books and you'll find answers.

It's an excellent program.

[GIMP] has many capabilities. It can be used as a simple paint program, an expert quality photo retouching program, an online batch processing system, a mass production image renderer, an image format converter, etc.

GIMP is expandable and extensible. It is designed to be augmented with plug-ins and extensions to do just about anything. The advanced scripting interface allows everything from the simplest task to the most complex image manipulation procedures to be easily scripted.[1]

In short, GIMP can be used for all of your graphic needs, and if a function is missing from GIMP you can browse through the registry of plugins available at *http://registry .gimp.org/list_content* to extend the functionality of GIMP.

There is a learning curve for those who haven't used a photo-editing package before, and even for those who might be used to another package (see Figure 7.1). GIMPshop

Figure 7.1 Options for editing photos in GIMP

(*http://www.gimpshop.com*) is available for those who learned on Photoshop®. It is a modified version of GIMP with menus and an interface like those used by Photoshop®.

If your library isn't looking for a graphic editing application, then think about providing your patrons with access to GIMP from your public machines. We are always looking for ways to improve the services we offer our patrons, while staying within our budget; this is a way to provide your patrons with a previously unavailable service at no extra cost to the library.

Desktop publishing

Another way to offer better services at no extra cost is to use Scribus (*http://www.scribus.net*) to produce a library newsletter. Scribus is an open source desktop publishing application. It comes ready with everything you need to create professional looking documents.

In addition to newsletters, you can use Scribus for creating support manuals, flyers and promotional materials for your library. The extensive online documentation and active community make it easy to find help as you learn to use Scribus. Scribus makes creating a library newsletter as easy as drag and drop; see Figure 7.2.

Despite all of this support and power, libraries and many other organizations have yet to discover Scribus. A survey of 977 librarians found only one using Scribus, and she was only using the application at home. This does not mean that Scribus cannot be used in libraries; it just means that Scribus hasn't been marketed in the library arena and has been overlooked.

Figure 7.2 Scribus

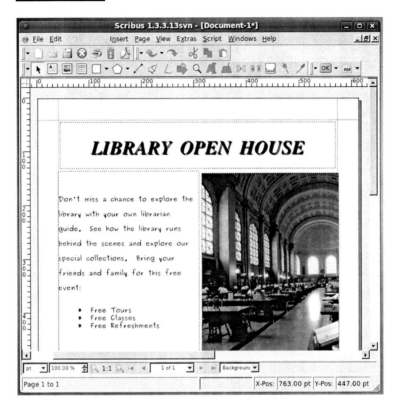

7.2 Open source in the real world: Scribus

Clay Fouts, Managing Editor of *Lion & Serpent*, a quarterly journal
Sekhet-Maat Lodge, representing Ordo Templi Orientis
Portland OR, USA

Why did you decide to use Scribus in your organization?

Because of budgetary constraints and the ideological preferences of much of our membership, we tend to use FOSS [free open source software] projects to fulfill our technical needs. Our extensive website incorporates

MediaWiki, Apache, MySQL, WordPress and other packages to manage and deliver content.

This trend continued when we developed a need for desktop publishing software. Our desire for proper color management, high quality font rendering, and vector graphics led us to a choice between Scribus and TeX. While TeX's descriptive language and maturity appeal to my programmer's mind, we thought Scribus' graphical interface and similarity to other desk-top publishing (DTP) software would make it easier for others to pick up the layout job in the future.

How are you using Scribus in your organization?

We originally started using it to produce the layout of our journal, *Lion & Serpent*. However, since using it for that purpose we have also used it to design all sorts of printed materials, including business cards, ceremony missals and the like.

How long have you been using Scribus in your organization?

Nine months.

Did you have any trouble implementing Scribus in your organization?

It is still young software, so is not as feature-rich as, say, InDesign. Because the more powerful features are in the newer, development versions (we currently use the 1.3.5.1 release), we also tend to run into instability and the occasional bug one is likely to find in bleeding-edge software. I haven't run into any show-stoppers, however.

What was the process of switching from proprietary to open source like?

Our previous layout person had used Adobe's InDesign, and there's no tool to translate those files used to create earlier journal volumes into Scribus' format. This meant we had to start over from scratch, more or less, and rebuild our template set in the new format.

However, since Scribus stores its documents in structured XML files, it's now possible to use versioning tools, like Git, to store branches and checkpoint revisions of documents with minimal fuss. We can experiment with a particular layout and, if we decide we don't like it, later easily revert to a previous revision.

Did you have any help installing, migrating to, or setting up Scribus?

I'm an IT professional, and we have a helpful member who formerly worked at a digital print shop to advise us on how to handle the inordinately confusing process of preparing our documents for printing.

What do you think of Scribus now?

It's actually so pleasing to use that I'm now glad we chose it over TeX. Being on one of their support mailing lists, it appears that members of the development team are managing the evolution of Scribus very well. The small but growing community is responsive to user inquiries. We now will not have to worry about diminished access to our templates and other DTP raw materials because of reliance on expensive proprietary software.

What do others in your organization say about Scribus?

In addition to our local membership, we have subscribers from around the world who read *Lion & Serpent*. Even though we distribute the online version at no charge, people specifically order subscriptions to the paper version for the careful reproductions of the beautiful artwork we publish. Response to the layout, design and production quality has been universally positive.

Are there any screenshots, documentation or features about your use of Scribus online or in library journals that we should look at?

You can find our online archive of issues at *http://sekhetmaat.com/Journal/*. All of volume 14 has been designed in Scribus.

One thing to keep in mind is that the images in the online digital version are compressed, to conserve bandwidth and to protect our visual artists' works from being distributed in a form suitable for mass production.

Anything else you want us to know about Scribus or your process of switching to Scribus?

Technical expertise, while helpful, is not necessary in order to use Scribus successfully. However, some very standard DTP functionality (font management and imposition are the most obvious) is still not directly supported from within Scribus and requires the use of other tools. Using these less refined and often command line programs would likely present a challenge for those with less tech savvy.

Although Scribus remains relatively unknown to the larger publishing industry, a growing number of non-profit and commercial organizations are using it for publishing a variety of documents, including magazines, books and marketing material. EASTeight magazine uses Scribus for its monthly publication delivered to 15,000 homes in London. Full Circle, an electronic magazine for Ubuntu users (a Linux-based operating system), is published monthly as an interactive PDF to the web. An increasing list of other titles published using the software is available on the Scribus Public Wiki.[2]

As with the other applications listed in this book, installing Scribus on your patrons stations is a great way to offer a service that was previously unavailable (and unaffordable) to your patrons.

Audio editing

Print products are not the only way to expand our library offerings; why not create a podcast? Libraries around the globe have started to offer free podcasts to their patrons to promote their collections, library events and the community. The New York Public Library has done an amazing job with podcasts at their library (see *http://www.nypl.org/voices/ audio-video*), but you do not have to be a large library system to be able to produce your own library show.

7.3 Open source in the real world: Audacity

Robin Stiles, Library Media Specialist, and Kristin Veenema, English Teacher
Staples High School Library Media Center
Westport CT, USA

Why did you decide to use Audacity in your library?

It is free. It has been promoted, downloaded and supported by our Information and Technology Literacy (ITL) department.

How are you using Audacity in your library?

It is loaded on 29 desktops on the main floor of the Library Media Center. It is loaded on 60+ laptops in the Library Media Center. We provide microphones and headphones that our students are able to check out and use. When teachers ask students to make a presentation, some do say that you can communicate your knowledge and research in a variety of ways. One of those options is to use Audacity.

How long have you been using Audacity in your library?

We have been using Audacity for three years. It was first introduced at our 'Summer ITL Institute' three years ago and each attendee received a microphone under their seat 'Oprah' style!

Did you have any trouble implementing Audacity in your library?

We needed to download a LAME MP3 encoder and keep it in the audacity file to be able to export files as .mp3 files.

What was the process of switching from proprietary to open source like?

We actually have only ever used Audacity.

Did you have any help installing, migrating to, or setting up Audacity?

Our tech department staff installed the software on all of our machines and are always available for training and support.

What do you think of Audacity now?

I think it is pretty cool. It's on my list of summer to-dos to record older family members and their memories to save for my kids. With this last class that I worked with I saw a change in their demeanor when they listened to their own voice, literally and figuratively.

What do others in your library say about Audacity?

Mac users of course prefer Mac software but we predominantly use PCs for instruction at Staples. Teachers who are podcasting more in the classroom use either Audacity (PC) or Podcast Capture (Mac) and upload files to their websites, wikis or Blackboard. With most technology it is not really the tool that you use but the goal in the learning that delivers the expected outcome of high level critical thinking.

Are there any screenshots, documentation or features about your use of Audacity online or in library journals that we should look at?

Students were asked to take an act of *The Crucible*, and write a script of lines that echoed each line with what they thought the main characters were really thinking and feeling. They were to record their reading of the actual lines interspersed with their thoughts of the character's thoughts or 'echoes of thought.' They were then to take a digital image of a tableau of their scene and link the podcast to their tableau image. They used Audacity to change their tone, depth of their voice and so on. Some made a female voice sound male or vice versa depending on the part they read. Shy, quiet students emerged with stronger voices. Group work enhanced the problem based learning; delving into the character's thoughts was challenging and different from previous assignments.

Anything else you want us to know about Audacity or your process of switching to Audacity?

You really should try to save your podcast as .mp3 to compress the size of the file because the .wav files can be large and sometimes too big depending on where you might want to save them.

Librarian and professor Michael Stephens introduces librarians to podcasting with Audacity (*http://audacity .sourceforge.net*):

> Audacity offers a no-cost audio recording solution that includes an intuitive interface and a small learning curve. Audio files recorded in Audacity can be saved as MP3, the standard podcast file format, or in other file formats as needed. MP3, which works on iPods and many other portable media players and CD players, is a file type that allows reasonable quality and a reasonable file size.[3]

Audacity is the tool of choice for many podcasters due to its powerful nature and the fact that it is free and open source.

Figure 7.3 Audacity

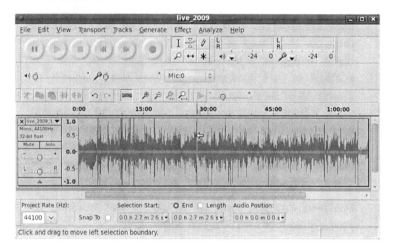

Using Audacity you can record, edit, splice and enhance your podcasts. This means you need only one tool to record and prepare your podcasts for publication. Audacity provides you with all of the tools necessary for creating podcasts; see Figure 7.3.

Screencasting

As a visual learner, I find video tutorials to be a great help when learning new software, or anything new for that matter. Providing your patrons with screencasts is a great way to help visual learners at your library with the various products that the library offers.

A screencast is simply a video recording of your computer screen, for example a tutorial for using the library website. You turn on your screencasting software and then navigate through the library site and narrate your movements. The screencasting software captures your movements and your voice and creates a video that you can then publish on the web.

CamStudio (*http://camstudio.org*) is an open source application that will help you create these screencasts on Windows, and recordmydesktop (*http://recordmydesktop .sourceforge.net*) is the solution if you are on a Linux operating system. Both these applications are extremely easy to use. Simply start up the application, choose the region you want to record on your screen and click the record button (see figures 7.4 and 7.5). Once your videos are recorded you can preview them in the application's viewer.

The Northeast Kansas Library System (NEKLS)[4] makes great use of screenscasts (*http://www.nexpresslibrary .org/category/tutorial/*) as training agents for their member libraries. These videos go along with text documentation they have written in order to make it easy for all types of learners to get the most out of their open source integrated library system, Koha (*http://koha-community.org*).

Figure 7.4 RecordMyDesktop records your actions as you navigate around your computer

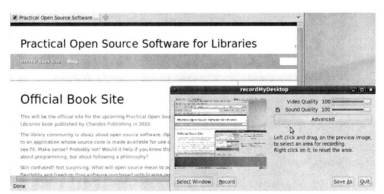

Figure 7.5 CamStudio provides you with details about your recording as you record your actions

7.4 Open source in the real world: RecordMyDesktop

Mark Osborne, Deputy Principal
Albany Senior High School Library
North Shore City, New Zealand

Why did you decide to use recordMyDesktop in your library?

We wanted to record screencasts to show users how to use features of the catalogue.

How are you using recordMyDesktop in your library?

Recording screencasts for the OPAC and software applications in use in our school.

How long have you been using recordMyDesktop in your library?

About 12 months.

Did you have any trouble implementing recordMyDesktop in your library?

No. Once we made sure the microphone was connected properly it was easy.

Did you have any help installing, migrating to, or setting up recordMyDesktop?

No. I installed it myself.

What do you think of recordMyDesktop now?

It's good. I will continue to use it.

What do others in your library say about recordMyDesktop?

The screencasts are extremely helpful and most people's preferred way of learning how to do something.

See screencasts created with recordMyDesktop online at *http://wikieducator.org/Albany_Senior_High_School/ICTs.*

Conclusion

Using the tools in this chapter you could set up a public media station within your library for little or no cost. Using an older or donated machine running Ubuntu, you can easily install all of the applications listed here (and more) and allow your patrons to start creating their very own movies, podcasts and newsletters.

Notes

1. 'Introduction to GIMP.' *GIMP*, 2009. *http://www.gimp.org/about/introduction.html.*
2. Harper, Eliot. 'Scribus: open source desktop publishing.' *Seybold Report: Analyzing Publishing Technologies* 9, no. 1 (January 8, 2009): 7–14.

3. Stephens, Michael. 'All About Podcasting.' *Library Media Connection* 25, no. 5 (February 2007): 54–57.
4. Please note, that while NEKLS makes great use of screencasts, they do not use either of the tools mentioned in this chapter.

Open source on the web

More and more librarians are being asked to join the ranks of the information technology staff. When I started in libraries I was in charge of the library websites. It was unthinkable that a librarian would have the skills, the desire, or the time for such a task. Now, with the prevalence of technology and the ever-shrinking library budgets, more and more librarians are stepping into the role of webmaster and, to do the job right, you need the right tools.

On the plus side, with the advent of the read/write web there are plenty of tools available for non developers to use to help create their websites, and many of them are open source.

Getting files onto the web

Before you start your website, you need at least one tool to help you transfer files from your computer to the web server. This process is called FTP or file transfer protocol. For this process you will need an FTP program; FileZilla (*http://filezilla-project.org*) is one of the popular choices among libraries. It is a favorite because it installs on nearly every operating system, making it easy to find the right version for you environment.

8.1 Open source in the real world: FileZilla

Rick Mason, Acquisitions Assistant
Blackmore Library, Capital University
Columbus OH, USA

Why did you decide to use FileZilla in your library?

I have used it for years for maintaining websites; when I need to FTP, it is the first program I go to.

How are you using FileZilla in your library?

The selection process for library materials from our prime vendor gives the acquisitions department files of MARC records on the vendor's server. We download the files, use other software (MarcEdit) to combine and prepare the files to be uploaded into our ILS.

How long have you been using FileZilla in your library?

I have been using FileZilla for this task for about a year; I have used it for a variety of other purposes for nearly eight years.

Did you have any trouble implementing FileZilla in your library?

There is a certain resistance to open source for some people; there is a feeling that 'you get what you pay for.' Once it becomes clear that it does the job effectively, that attitude generally softens.

What was the process of switching from proprietary to open source like?

For me, liberating. When I first tried FileZilla, I had been using a proprietary program that was several versions out of date, and couldn't be installed on additional machines. Having a program that was frequently updated and could be set up on all the computers I needed it on was a great change.

Did you have any help installing, migrating to, or setting up FileZilla?

Nope... not necessary with our environment. I have installed the program and trained quite a few people in its use, though. The PortableApps (*http://portableapps.com*) version makes this very easy, because the program can be configured for the remote server access in advance.

What do you think of FileZilla now?

It is still the primary tool for my FTP needs; if I find another program that does it better (and that includes the benefits of open source) I would switch. That is just the nature of the 'toolbox' concept of software – keep the best tool for the job at hand. That I have used it as my primary FTP software for this long is a great compliment to those who maintain it.

What do others in your library say about FileZilla?

FTP is not a high-profile or conversation-dominating thing for most people; those who use it recognize the benefits.

Anything else you want us to know about FileZilla or your process of switching to FileZilla?

Just this: the best approach to software is the toolbox analogy I referred to earlier. Just as most people have more than one screwdriver, using the one that will best serve the job at hand, we should seek out software and try it out enough to find out how well it performs. When a new situation presents itself, hopefully the software is already in our 'toolbox,' waiting to be used.

FileZilla displays the content of your local machine and the web server side by side, making it easy for you to drag files from your computer onto the web server. Files on the server can be modified simply by clicking with your right mouse button on the title and choosing an option from the menu that appears. Often a web application will require that a folder has specific permissions, a process once reserved for the IT staff. Using the right click menu in FileZilla you can choose 'change permissions' and choose the options required by the software you are installing. You can also move files around and rename them using right click and drag and drop functionality within FileZilla; see Figure 8.1.

Like most of the applications mentioned so far, FileZilla has an active developer community, so there are lots of ways to find support, tips and documentation, many updates and improved functionality.

Figure 8.1   FileZilla

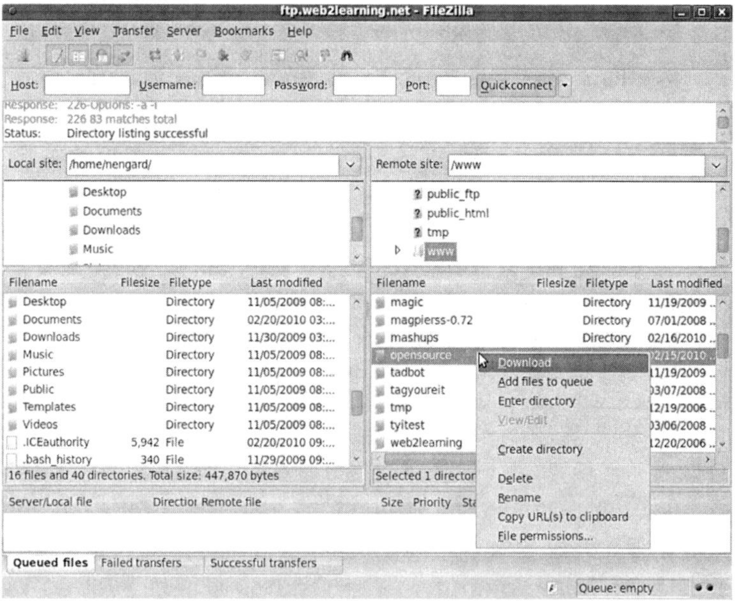

Content management

Now that you can upload files to the web, you need something to upload. Many libraries have been choosing to use a content management system to design their library sites. A content management system is almost like a website in a box; it has everything you need to build and maintain your website without having any formal training or web development skills. There are currently two popular open source content management systems in the library world: Joomla (*http://www.joomla.org*) and Drupal (*http://www .drupal.org*). Your basic content management system provides you with the necessary tools for creating pages for your site without having to know HTML or any other programming language.

8.2 Open source in the real world: Joomla

Jason Griffey, Head of Library Information Technology
Lupton Library, University of TN at Chattanooga
Chattanooga TN, USA

Why did you decide to use Joomla in your library?

We were in the midst of a website redesign, and the decision for a content management system came down to either Joomla or Drupal. The decision to use Joomla was driven by the fact that it was easier for a single, part-time developer (me) to create a theme and move the content into. Drupal is great, but was out of my reach given the time constraints. Joomla was much faster to develop for.

How are you using Joomla in your library?

We are using Joomla to drive our library's website, with the exception of our database page and catalog.

How long have you been using Joomla in your library?

We've been fully on Joomla since early 2007.

Did you have any trouble implementing Joomla in your library?

Other than time constraints, no. Being an academic library, there was of course a committee involved, but I was able to discuss the benefits of open source and convince anyone who doubted.

What was the process of switching from proprietary to open source like?

Very easy. Detail oriented, but overall the process was a smooth one.

Did you have any help installing, migrating to, or setting up Joomla?

Nope, the development, installation and so on was all done by me. The rest of the librarians helped with the migration, but we had no outside help.

What do you think of Joomla now?

I still prefer it to our old, flat-file solution, but it has its issues. The way it deals with content and menus can be non-intuitive for those not used to developing on Joomla. But it's still a robust platform.

What do others in your library say about Joomla?

Mostly they are happy with it. There are some problems with the creation of entirely new sections of the site... updating existing information is easy, but the creation of new sections can be non-intuitive.

With Drupal, the different areas of the site are broken into 'tasks' and 'modules' (see Figure 8.2). A task is essentially the function of the page, what the page does. A module is more a section of the site, for example 'Events,' 'Blog,' or 'User.' In Joomla content is sorted into 'Menus,' 'Content,' and 'Components' (see Figure 8.3). Each of these areas houses sections of the site that you are able to alter and customize. Of the two, I find the Joomla administration area a bit easier to navigate, but both could use a librarian's touch. In the end, both have their strong points and their weak points; my recommendation is to try out both using the demos on the opensourceCMS website (*http://opensourcecms .com*) to find the one that works the best for your needs.

To see what these tools can do, both Joomla and Drupal maintain showcases of sites using their product (*http:// community.joomla.org/showcase/ and http://drupal.org/cases*).

Figure 8.2   Administration area on GPLLA.org, which is powered by Drupal

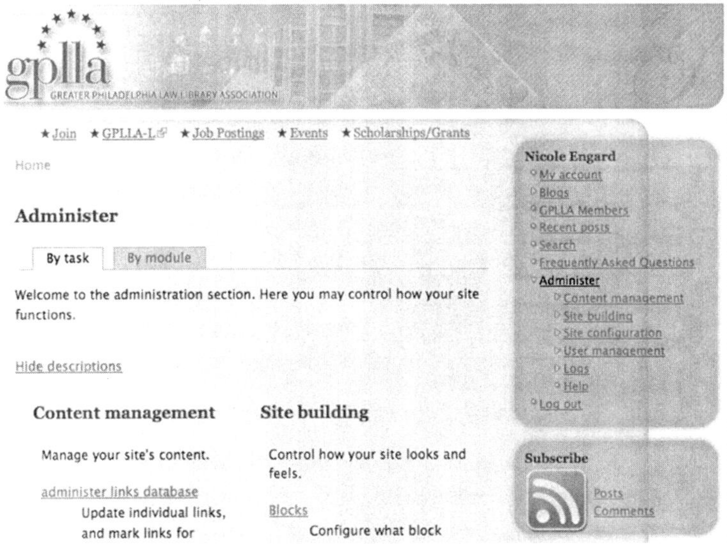

Figure 8.3 The Joomla administration area

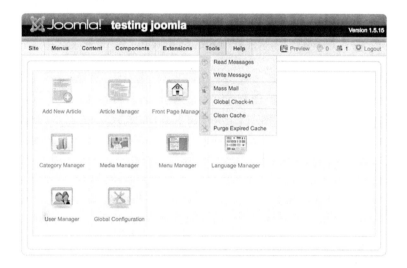

8.3 Open source in the real world: Drupal

Paula Gray-Overtoom, Information Systems Librarian
Monroe County Public Library
Bloomington IN, USA

Why did you decide to use Drupal in your library?

We wanted to have a content management system for our intranet. We were using Macromedia/Adobe Contribute with templates to guide staff in creating content, but it just wasn't dynamic enough. We wanted to be able to have staff blogs for different departments and allow all staff to contribute to the intranet. With Drupal we didn't have to worry about being able to afford licenses for all of our staff.

How are you using Drupal in your library?

We are using Drupal for our intranet. We have departmental blogs, post documents and staff meeting information. It is the way we communicate within and between service areas.

How long have you been using Drupal in your library?

We have had Drupal installed for about a year, but have only moved all staff to it as our new intranet face for about a month.

Did you have any trouble implementing Drupal in your library?

It took a while for me to learn how to install modules and other technical aspects of Drupal, but the online documentation is good and very accessible. Staff picked up on using Drupal very quickly. We had one-hour training sessions for most staff to go over the basics of updating their account information and posting blog entries. Staff have transitioned to Drupal with very few issues. Most of them are really happy that they can now edit pages without having to use Contribute.

What was the process of switching from proprietary to open source like?

We use open source for our web server anyway, so the transition for Drupal was pretty easy. We were behind in our version of Contribute anyway because of the licensing fees, so it was much better to be able to move to an up-to-date piece of software. From using Red Hat, I was already used to going online to find answers to my problems and actually find that I like that better than having to go to a proprietary company with the hope that they will be responsive to my needs.

Did you have any help installing, migrating to, or setting up Drupal?

I set up Drupal on my own.

What do you think of Drupal now?

I really like it. It works well for our needs and usually when I have a software need, I go search through the contributed modules for Drupal and find a module that does what I want. I think that one of the most interesting parts of open source is that someone is always developing something to fill a need.

What do others in your library say about Drupal?

Everybody seems to like it. Some staff weren't sure about it at first, but I've gotten really positive feedback. Staff are glad that they are able to easily search the site and find what they need.

Anything else you want us to know about Drupal or your process of switching to Drupal?

Drupal really does work great for an intranet. We have been able to create books for various manuals that keep documents organized, use forms for sending work requests to IT or facilities, and communicate easily with blogs. It is much easier to update information using Drupal than any other system I've used, excluding emacs.

A recent popular addition to the Drupal showcase is the official White House website (*http://www.whitehouse .gov*).[1] A more obvious pairing is the use of Joomla by Linux.com (*http://www.linux.com*) because of its open source focus.

New on the library content management front is MaiaCMS (*http://maiacms.org*), designed by the Howard County Library system in Maryland, USA. MaiaCMS was designed by and for librarians making it a very promising option for library websites. I have worked with both Joomla and Drupal and my top complaint is that the administrative user interface seems more complicated than it needs to be. This is why MaiaCMS is so exciting to me; it is a tool designed by librarians for librarians, so the menu system is nicely organized and easy to navigate (see Figure 8.4), and modules that librarians need are part of the standard install instead of available solely as plugins.

Figure 8.4 The librarian created administration area of MaiaCMS

8.4 Open source in the real world: MaiaCMS

Danny Bouman, Web Developer
Howard County Library
Columbia MD, USA

Why did you decide to develop MaiaCMS for your library?

I decided to develop MaiaCMS because the library was interested in designing a new website and a content management system was necessary to allow non-technical staff to contribute and maintain the content on the site. I had explored several existing CMS options such as Joomla and Drupal, but I was just not happy at the time with how complex they were and how much tweaking would be needed to simplify them for our users. Creating MaiaCMS from scratch gave me the platform to create a truly customized system that would be well suited to meet the exact needs of Howard County Library.

How are you using MaiaCMS in your library?

MaiaCMS is currently our public website (*http://hclibrary.org*) and is entirely maintained by our Marketing Department.

How long have you been using MaiaCMS in your library?

We have been using MaiaCMS for a little over a year now.

What was the process of switching from proprietary to open source like?

We did not have a proprietary system before. Although it was developed by an outside web design company, we always had access to modify the website as we needed.

What do you think of MaiaCMS now?

MaiaCMS continues to work extremely well for Howard County Library due in large part to the fact that it was developed for Howard County Library. If I were to go back and do it over again, however, I would choose to start with Joomla or Drupal as a foundation rather than developing a new system from scratch. I found that as I was releasing MaiaCMS to the public, I was being forced to replicate many of the features already existing in Joomla and Drupal.

What do others in your library say about MaiaCMS?

The Marketing Department has mentioned that they find it extremely easy to use. Many staff members have commented that the simplistic design makes it easy to navigate.

From a developer perspective, I would say that it is difficult to install and configure due to the current lack of documentation.

Are there any screenshots, documentation or features about your use of MaiaCMS online or in library journals that we should look at?

Documentation (when it is written) and screenshots can be found at *http://maiacms.org*.

Features of MaiaCMS include:

- simple and intuitive design
- ability to easily create and administer forms
- innovative system for managing site contacts
- components for sending out newsletters, adding promotional items, making announcements, and adding job openings.

Anything else you want us to know about MaiaCMS or your process of switching to MaiaCMS?

All of the code is freely available at *http://maiacms.org* to anyone who wishes to use it. Due to the project still being in its infancy, site administrators will need to be familiar with PHP in order to install and configure the product.

The one drawback to MaiaCMS is that it is currently only being used at one library, so there is no active community to go to for support and no documentation available online. I would recommend that librarians keep MaiaCMS on their radar, but not make the leap to implementing it in their library until there is a bit more activity around it.

Often overlooked as a content management system is WordPress (*http://wordpress.org*). Originally used as a blogging platform, recent upgrades to WordPress have made it a viable alternative to the systems usually thought of as the top open source content management systems (see Table 8.1 for a basic CMS comparison). WordPress comes with all of the trademarks of an amazing open source application: active community, strong user base, extensive documentation and the ability to extend functionality with user-developed plugins. In fact, WordPress is found on nearly three times as many big sites[2] as Drupal (which is used three times more than Joomla).[3]

Table 8.1 Comparison of content management systems

	Joomla	Drupal	MaiaCMS	WordPress
Premade templates	Yes	Yes	No	Yes
Wiki functionality	w/plugin	w/plugin	No	w/plugin
Blog functionality	Yes	Yes	No	Yes
Support options	Forums	Forums	Mailing	Forums
Library community	Yes	Yes	No	Yes
Extensions	Yes	Yes	No	Yes
Multi-user management	Yes	Yes	Yes	Yes
OPAC plugin	No	SOPAC2	No	Scriblio
Built-in search	Yes	Yes	Yes	Yes
RSS feeds	Yes	Yes	Yes	Yes

One of the biggest selling points for WordPress to those who are unfamiliar with installing web applications is its five-second install. You are asked a few short questions, click submit and you have a WordPress site up and running. You can then walk through the easy-to-understand 'Settings' section and customize some of the ways people will interact with your new site. The thing that takes the most time is finding the theme you like best. When teaching WordPress to fellow librarians, this is the part of the class that always takes the longest, a true testament to how easy it is to learn (see Figure 8.5) and use WordPress to manage your entire library website.

Consulting with colleagues

When choosing to use a new or unfamiliar tool, it is always handy to have access to colleagues who have gone before

| Figure 8.5 | The administration panel on the official book site (*http://opensource.web2learning.net*), powered by WordPress |

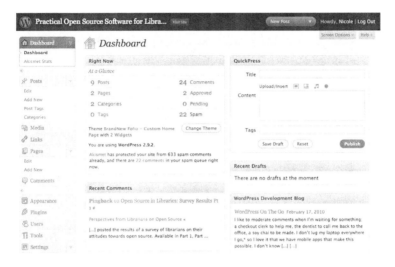

8.5 Open source in the real world: WordPress

Susan Bryant, Outreach Librarian
Morrill Public Library
Hiawatha KS, USA

Why did you decide to use WordPress in your library?

WordPress gives us control over the content and look of our website without having to do a lot of complex HTML coding or waiting until a remote webmaster handles it for us. In other words, we don't have to be tech wizards to have a professional looking site.

How are you using WordPress in your library?

We use it for our library website (*http://www.hiawathalibrary.org*).

How long have you been using WordPress in your library?

Since 2006.

Did you have any trouble implementing WordPress in your library? What was the process of switching from proprietary to open source like? Did you have any help installing, migrating to, or setting up WordPress?

Our WordPress website is part of the My Kansas Library on the Web (KLOW) project (*http://www.mykansaslibrary .org*), so our site is provided by the State Library of Kansas and hosted by the Northeast Kansas Library System (NeKLS) (*http://www.nekls.org*) at no cost to our library. The NeKLS technical staff very capably handled the details of setting up our site, domain name, and so on. They also provided training on using WordPress, and this support continues today. On the last Friday of each month they host 'Website Workdays' in their computer lab so librarians can get advice and help on changing themes, adding plugins, editing theme features, and so on. And NeKLS makes great coffee!

What do you think of WordPress now?

I like it a lot. My pet peeve is websites that are not kept up to date, and with WordPress the user interface is so simple that I log in to the dashboard almost every day and tweak something. Also, it's easy to have more than one staff member contributing to the site.

We also like the idea that we can 'redecorate' our website anytime by changing themes, adding different text or picture widgets to the sidebars, and so on. We currently use the 'Garland Theme' and like the custom colors feature to make seasonal changes.

What do others in your library say about WordPress?

Our staff think of our website as a resource for answering reference questions, so we have loaded it with links useful to our patrons and us. Our staff sometimes suggest adding new links and deleting unused links to make the website more useful, and I think they like it that their suggestions can be implemented immediately.

Anything else you want us to know about WordPress or your process of switching to WordPress?

The assistance and ongoing support of the KLOW team was of great consequence to our decision to use WordPress.

you and been successful. This is why there are three communities you should be aware of before choosing a content management system.

If you are interested in Joomla, you might want to check out the Joomla in Libraries (*http://www.joomlainlibrary.com*) community. This site focuses on libraries that have or want to use Joomla to manage their library site or intranet. The amount of helpful content on this site is amazing. You can find tutorials, examples from other libraries, a discussion board and more.

For those wanting to learn more about Drupal, there is the Drupalib (*http://drupalib.interoperating.info*) community. This site is also a wealth of information for those using or wanting to use Drupal to manage sites within their library. From here you can access other Drupal libraries by participating in the mailing list or the forums, you can see other libraries that are using Drupal in the showcase and you can access tips and tricks by subscribing to the blog.

Finally, if you are interested in WordPress, the community for you is wp4lib (*http://www.webjunction.org/706*). This community consists of message boards, a wiki and a discussion list. With access to other libraries that have already implemented WordPress your migration will be that much easier.

Wikis

Some libraries will forego a content management system in favor of a wiki. A wiki is simply a website that multiple people can edit. One of the most well known open source wiki applications is MediaWiki (*http://www.mediawiki.org*), the software that powers Wikipedia (*http://www.wikipedia.org*). MediaWiki has a long established record for handling heavily trafficked websites with ease, which is why it is commonly used by librarians to power their intranets, subject guides and sometimes entire websites.

8.6 Open source in the real world: MediaWiki

Garry Collum, Systems Coordinator
Kenton County Public Library
Covington KY, USA

Why did you decide to use MediaWiki in your library?

Kenton County Public Library (KCPL) at one time had 'ready reference' questions and frequently asked reference questions, Qs & As, stored in an ILS vendor's electronic version of Community Resources.

This product was difficult to update and used MARC records as its data format. The IT department wanted to find a product that was easy to update and that all staff could access.

MediaWiki was chosen and at first only contained these two information sources. However, after using MediaWiki for a few weeks, it seemed to be a natural progression just to move the entire intranet to a wiki format.

Before installing MediaWiki, the staff of KCPL would send all of their documents to the IT department to be placed on the intranet. The IT department wanted to find a way to eliminate the 'middle man.'

How are you using MediaWiki in your library?

We use MediaWiki for our intranet.

How long have you been using MediaWiki in your library?

We installed MediaWiki on October 11, 2006.

Did you have any trouble implementing MediaWiki in your library?

The installation was simple, but you do need to have someone who has some familiarity with Apache, MySQL and Linux file permissions. The hardest part of the installation was configuring the wiki options. Not the process of configuration itself, but how and what to configure (namespaces, users and so on.)

What was the process of switching from proprietary to open source like?

The most time-consuming process of switching to MediaWiki was moving documents into the wiki. We actually didn't move from proprietary to open source; we moved from web pages, or MS Office documents, to wiki format.

Did you have any help installing, migrating to, or setting up MediaWiki?

We used the online documentation to set up and configure the wiki.

What do you think of MediaWiki now?

It fits our needs perfectly.

What do others in your library say about MediaWiki?

The staff who use MediaWiki to update their pages, or who have created their own departmental pages, like the product. MediaWiki is easy to use, but it is not intuitive. Staff who infrequently update pages seem to need a refresher on how to create or update pages and the tags that are used for formatting.

MediaWiki offers a series of settings to allow you to decide how you want people to interact with your website. It is a common misconception that all wikis are open for anyone to edit; as the site administrator you can decide if a password is required for editing. Since wikis keep a complete history of edits, a common practice is to give each staff member their own login so all their edits are recorded. This makes it easy to find the right person to contact if you have a question about a particular edit. Also, since a complete history is kept, it is always an option to revert to an older version of the page, making it less daunting to allow anyone on the staff access to edit pages; see Figure 8.6.

One drawback of MediaWiki, and many other wikis as well, is that the interface can sometimes be less than intuitive. While a WYSIWYG (what you see is what you get) editor is available to make editing the pages simpler, the wiki syntax can sometimes still confuse people. It can also be difficult to know where to go to edit a page or to revert to a previous edit. That said, the documentation for MediaWiki is extensive and can easily be searched for the solution to your particular problem.

Figure 8.6 Editing the open source page on the Library Success Wiki[4] powered by MediaWiki

Conclusion

These web applications are simply a small sampling of the open source alternatives available to help with managing your library website. The key is to try out a few options before making a choice and always remember to contact your colleagues around the world to see how they are using the applications, why they chose them and if they are happy with their choice. Also remember that the opensourceCMS website (*http://opensourcecms.com*) and others like it allow you to test drive open source web applications before actually pitching them to your library staff or installing them yourself.

Notes

1. Buytaert, Dries. 'Whitehouse.gov Using Drupal.' *Dries Buytaert*, October 25, 2009. *http://buytaert.net/whitehouse-gov-using-drupal*.
2. 'Big sites' is defined by Alexa's top 10,000 most popular websites. See *http://www.alexa.com*.
3. Geller, Tom. 'Drupal Runs Three Times as Many Top Sites as the Next CMS.' *Tom Geller's Latest Thing*, January 18, 2010. *http://tomgeller.com/content/drupal-runs-three-times-many-top-sites-next-cms*.
4. See *http://www.libsuccess.org/index.php?title=Open_Source_Software*.

Open sourcing collections

When asked what they think of when they think of libraries, most people will offer 'books' as their first answer. As librarians, we know that our buildings house all types of collections, which are certainly not limited to books. We also know that if they cannot be found with an easy search via the web, then our patrons will never know about the amazing collections housed in our libraries. The following open source tools will help you make your digital collections visible to your patrons via the web.

Digital collections

Digital collections can come in many shapes and forms. Some are used to keep an archive of publications produced by your institution, some are provided as a way to keep a history of the community, and some provide files on a specific topic. Whatever your digital collection might be used for or made up of, there is an open source application that will help index and provide the necessary data.

Greenstone (*http://www.greenstone.org*) is a digital library application that allows for the distribution of data via the internet and/or digital media such as a CD ROM or DVD. This flexibility has made it extremely popular worldwide. I was able to install the application and create a website for my collection in less than an hour (see Figure 9.1).

Figure 9.1 Editing Dublin Core using the Greenstone Librarian interface

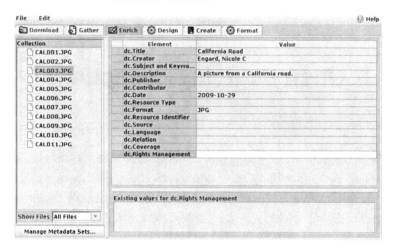

Using the Greenstone Librarian Interface you can easily browse for files on your local machine, network or the web and import them into your collection. Greenstone allows for many collections, each of which can be made up of documents, images, videos, audio files and more. Greenstone has also been developed with worldwide accessibility in mind.

9.1 Open source in the real world: Greenstone

Peter Stone, Technology Support Services Team Leader, and David Friggens, Systems Librarian
University of Waikato Library
Hamilton, New Zealand

Why did you decide to use Greenstone in your library?

We needed a digital collection manager that was robust and relatively easy to implement in a Linux system, and the Computer Science Department at University of Waikato develops and maintains Greenstone.

How are you using Greenstone in your library?

We are using Greenstone for two collections. The first collection is the *New Zealand Gazette*, which is provided commercially; we use Greenstone to manage the PDF documents locally. This was the original impetus for using Greenstone, as the provided proprietary software was not really fit for purpose.

The other collection is the parts of the *London Illustrated News* 1842–1902 that relate to New Zealand. This collection is publicly available and contains scanned images of the pages along with OCR text for searching.

We have some other local collections that we hope to make available using Greenstone in the near future.

How long have you been using Greenstone in your library?

Some five years (possibly six years). We are about to upgrade to the latest version.

Did you have any trouble implementing Greenstone in your library?

No.

What was the process of switching from proprietary to open source like?

It was a major improvement, as we gained control of how the collection(s) presented to the user and how services that the user might want were presented.

Did you have any help installing, migrating to, or setting up Greenstone?

No, we worked it out ourselves; however I do think the documentation for the upgrade version we are about to migrate to is far better that what we dealt with originally.

What do you think of Greenstone now?

It's a solid, reliable product.

What do others in your library say about Greenstone?

Where we have chosen to use Greenstone, they are happy. However, we have not progressed with customizations due to other work commitments.

The international Unicode character set is used throughout, so that documents in any language and character encoding can be imported (in fact, Greenstone can automatically detect the language and encoding of most documents). Collections of documents in Arabic, Chinese, Cyrillic, English, French, Spanish, German, Hindi and Maori are publicly available. The New Zealand Digital Library website (*http://nzdl.org*) hosts many of these, and the Greenstone website links to sites that contain further examples.

It makes little sense to have a collection whose content is in Chinese or Russian, but whose supporting text – instructions, navigation buttons, labels, images, help text, and so on – are in English. Consequently, the entire Greenstone interface has been translated into a range of languages, and the interface language can be changed by the user as they browse from the Preferences page.[1]

In addition to the freedom of organizing multimedia collections, Greenstone also offers customization of the interface and metadata formats. By default, Greenstone's user interface has a very clean look and feel, but many libraries want to make their digital library site look more like their traditional library site for branding purposes (see Figure 9.2). To get ideas of what kinds of customizations have been done, you can view the list of example collections on the Greenstone official site (*http://www.greenstone.org/examples*). Waikato

Figure 9.2 The Illustrated London News[2] on the University of Waikato website

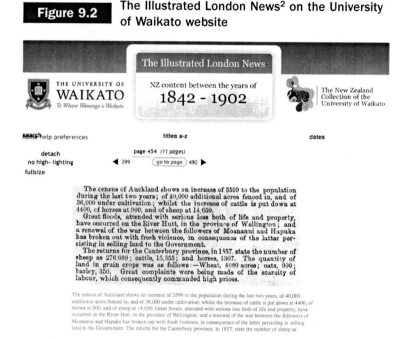

University manages its digital archive of the *Illustrated London News* (*http://digital.liby.waikato.ac.nz*) on Greenstone; see Figure 9.2.

Institutional repositories

Although Greenstone can be used for any type of digital collection, when it comes to storing data published by those within your institution, DSpace (*http://dspace.org*) seems to be the popular option.

The most common use of the DSpace software is by academic and research libraries as an open access repository for managing their faculty and student output. There are also many organizations using the software to host and manage subject based, dataset or media-based repositories.[3]

9.2 Open source in the real world: DSpace

Beth Tillinghast, Web Support Librarian and ScholarSpace
Project Manager
University of Hawaii at Manoa Library
Honolulu HI, USA

Why did you decide to use DSpace in your library?

Our Information Technology Division Head had seen the DSpace system, Deep Blue, working at the University of Michigan. We contacted them and discussed their repository and reviewed Deep Blue via a conference call. After looking at two other open source repository platforms, we decided that DSpace would best suit our needs. Part of that decision was based on the strong DSpace community support that was available.

How are you using DSpace in your library?

We are using the DSpace platform for our institutional repository, ScholarSpace (*https://scholarspace.manoa.hawaii.edu*). This repository houses the intellectual output from our faculty and students.

In addition we have just created another DSpace instance that we have named eVols. It will be used to house content that may not actually be the intellectual output from our university, but is content over which the UHM Library has guardianship. An example of this is our University of Hawaii Catalogs.

How long have you been using DSpace in your library?

We began working with the system in the late fall of 2006 and started adding small pilot projects to ScholarSpace in the spring of 2007.

Did you have any trouble implementing DSpace in your library?

No, but we are fortunate to have staff with the skills needed to tackle this kind of project.

What was the process of switching from proprietary to open source like?

We didn't make a switch from proprietary. We began our repository using open source. Our department, the Desktop Network Services, has had quite a bit of experience using open source software.

Did you have any help installing, migrating to, or setting up DSpace?

Our system administrator installed DSpace on one of our library servers, and we had one of our librarians with a good deal of technical skills configure it. They used the existing documentation from the DSpace website and didn't run into trouble during the implementation. The DSpace listservs provided answers to questions they had during that time.

What do you think of DSpace now?

We are quite happy with the system. Part of this is because of the DSpace user community and the upgrades and add-ons that are being created. They address the needs of repository managers and the system users.

What do others in your library say about DSpace?

Most people are very supportive. They understand the need for an institutional repository. Some of our librarians are very active in promoting this service.

In addition to the ability to store various different data types (documents, images, videos, audio recordings, and so on) DSpace also offers a series of add-ons or plugins (*http://dspace.org/add-ons-and-extensions/addons/*) to extend the functionality of the application. In true open source fashion, DSpace also allows for customization of look and feel and metadata formatting (see Figure 9.3).

Figure 9.3 The ScholarSpace web page at University of Hawaii at Manoa Library

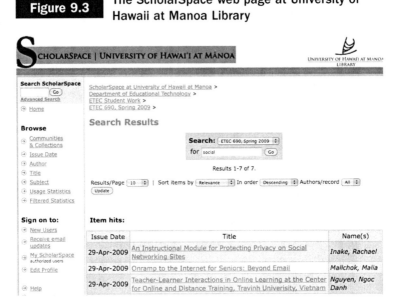

Like Greenstone, DSpace also allows for the creation of several different collections, which users can then browse or search through. This flexibility, a trademark of an open source application, is part of what makes this application the choice of so many institutions.

Community built collections

Greenstone and DSpace are well established tools for sharing digital collections with the outside world, but what about allowing the outside world to share its collections with us? Kete (*http://kete.net.nz*) turns the traditional digital library inside out by allowing the library to host and moderate the content added by community members.

9.3 Open source in the real world: Kete

Joann Ransom, Acting Head of Libraries
Horowhenua Library Trust
Levin, New Zealand

Why did you decide to use Kete in your library?

In 2005 we carried out an audit of arts, cultural and heritage resources in our district. We found that there is a large amount of material in private hands; 'shoeboxes under the bed' was how we viewed them. While some of it was destined to be given to historical societies most of it would not. However, almost all of it was available for display, copying and sharing so long as we gave the originals back.

We needed a digital repository that would be easy for the general public to add material to. The library's role would be to provide a forum, promote it and support the community to encourage the growth of the digital collection.

How are you using Kete in your library?

1. Kete has provided a way for our local heritage sector to digitise and make available their collections, without compromising the originals.

2. Kete has enabled us to digitise and make available 24/7 our vertical file collection of local material.

3. It has also allowed previously hidden or private local content to become available.

4. Kete has been a splendid marketing tool for the library. We do loads of public speaking, explaining how local groups and organisations can use Kete, both in terms of searching and contributing.

5. Kete has given us the excuse to draw people into the library and teach them IT skills. We ran regular working bees for volunteers to use staff

machines after hours to digitise the photograph collection of the local historical societies. In the process we have formed great relationships and taught many people IT skills.

How long have you been using Kete in your library?

We developed Kete during the latter half of 2006 and did a soft launch in March 2007, which allowed us to get 'seed content' in before the official launch in June 2007.

Did you have any trouble implementing Kete in your library?

None at all. We advertised in the paper for volunteers and were overwhelmed with help. Our community love helping build such a cool resource, and our heritage sector are delighted we have given them a way to make their collections available.

The large increase of volunteers popping into the library took a wee bit of getting used to for staff not directly involved in the project and who hadn't been exposed to the enthusiasm.

What was the process of switching from proprietary to open source like?

This was a new venture for us in terms of collecting informal content.

Did you have any help installing, migrating to, or setting up Kete?

Walter McGinnis from Katipo Communications in Wellington was the primary developer and does a splendid job making our vision a reality.

What do you think of Kete now?

Love it – and I fall in love with it all over again everytime I get to share it with people and see their reaction.

What do others in your library say about Kete?

Those who embrace the project and commit resources to market it in the community and actively encourage and support the creation of content get a lot more from Kete than those who expect it to populate itself. It takes time and effort to build an online community. I make sure I respond to new contributors and acknowledge their additions to Kete through comments, making gentle suggestions or editing out obvious mistakes. I also like to celebrate submissions by making them feature topics on the home page. Kete is not a silver bullet, but it is an amazing excuse to get out there and talk to every organisation, club and community group in your town – and build a great local resource while you are at it.

Joann Ransom writes about the process of choosing the name Kete for this community-built digital library:

> Echoing the Maori proverb of the three baskets, or kete, of knowledge, we called our concept Kete. We really like what the kete represents. We like that they are 'honest', practical items, woven from found materials, and that anyone can learn to weave one. We like that they are made from flax, which springs forth from Papatuanuku, the earth mother. We like the link between the flax and the weaver – the person who caressed and shaped the flax into a beautiful or useful object. We like that kete are usually given from 1 person to another, so linking people together, and that they are usually given to mark an occasion so there are stories that surround a kete. When a kete is used and taken from one occasion to another, the stories are being told and the history preserved. The kete is an appropriate metaphor for our digital library, and the various types of material it contains.[4]

With Kete, a library can set up the software on its servers and then open up the content-adding tools to its community members. The library hosting the Kete instance gets to define who the 'community members' are. If you work in a public library your community might be anyone with a library card or anyone in the world. If you are in an academic or school library, your community may only consist of students and professors.

The community then decides what kinds of content are added to the digital library (see Figure 9.4). This is a great way to collect all of the treasures hiding in your patrons' attics. Pieces of family histories are lost daily; with a tool like this available, community members can share their treasures without giving them up to the library. Kete Horowhenua (*http://horowhenua.kete.net.nz*) is the perfect example of how a community can get together to share their history with each other. Kete Horowhenua is a collection of digital resources managed by members of the community; see Figure 9.4.

Figure 9.4   Kete Horowhenua web page at Horowhenua Library Trust

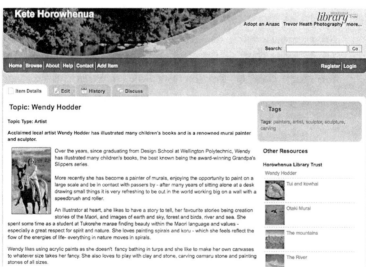

Baskets of knowledge

Between the library and the community there are many amazing collections worth sharing with others. One or all of these tools can be used to make collections accessible through the library website to the wider world.

Notes

1. Witten, Ian H., Matt Jones, David Bainbridge, Polly Cantlon, and Sally Jo Cunningham. 'Digital Libraries for Creative Communities.' *Digital Creativity* 15, no. 2 (June 2004): 110–125.
2. See *http://digital.liby.waikato.ac.nz*.
3. 'DSpace Use Case Examples.' *DSpace. http://dspace.org/use-case-examples/DSpace-Use-Cases.html*.
4. Ransom, Joann. 'Kete Horowhenua: the story of the district as told by its people.' *Kete.net.nz*, February 2008. *http://kete.net .nz/blog/documents/show/33-kete-horowhenua-the-story-of-the-district-as-told-by-its-people*.

Open source research tools

In addition to digital collections, libraries have many other resources to share online. Many library websites offer lists of links on specific topics, subject guides and even online workshops to help educate their patrons. As with every other area of the library, there are open source technologies to help us deliver these guides and classes in an efficient manner.

Subject guides

In my first job in a library I was in charge of managing the library's research links collection. This area of our site was very similar to the pages that academic libraries call subject guides. Whatever you might call them, these pages can be tedious to keep up to date if you are not using the right tool. In my library we were just using a series of static HTML pages that had to be updated regularly,[1] a practice not uncommon in libraries around the world.

Two open source tools that libraries have created to tackle this problem are SubjectsPlus (*http://www.subjectplus.com*) and Library à la Carte™ (*http://alacarte.library.oregonstate.edu*).

10.1 Open source in the real world: SubjectsPlus

Bryan P. Carson, Electronic Services Librarian and Technology Liaison to the Language Schools
Middlebury College
Middlebury VT, USA

Why did you decide to use SubjectsPlus in your library?

It is open source. It was easy to implement, lightweight and database-driven and it integrates well with other platforms.

How are you using SubjectsPlus in your library?

We use it for library subject guides and associating librarians contact info subject-specific content. We also use it for EZProxy integration with our subscription resources. It is also our main database (A–Z) list as well.

How long have you been using SubjectsPlus in your library?

I installed it in November 2007 and content has been gradually migrated into it over the 2008/09 academic year.

Did you have any trouble implementing SubjectsPlus in your library?

Not really. The open source community for this is growing and active. Andrew Darby (the lead developer) is very helpful. He is our 'Linus' or 'Dries.'

What was the process of switching from proprietary to open source like?

Conventional wisdom says that proprietary software is expensive but it saves your staff time and money, while open source is 'free' but it does still cost you in staff time. Not true! We have found that proprietary is expensive *and* costs you just as much in staff time and money, often more, because fewer folks can pitch in and help. So it was for us. The switch from content in a Microsoft product was met with enthusiasm. We were able to meet the usability needs of our users better. Changes and customizations are easy. Costs and time are down. User satisfaction is way up.

Did you have any help installing, migrating to, or setting up SubjectsPlus?

Our network administrators set up virtual server for it and set up security, so it can't bring down any other servers if it gets hacked. One of our web programmers looked for any obvious security issues in the code and sent them back to Andrew Darby for his prompt repair. All the customizations and other tweaking, I did myself.

What do you think of SubjectsPlus now?

I think it is excellent (and the price is right). Now that we have a critical mass of records, SubjectsPlus's ability to distribute the content creation lets us create and update guides very quickly. Additionally, it stores the data in a very structured way allowing our web programmers to create feeds for our website.

What do others in your library say about SubjectsPlus?

Everyone who sees the resulting interface loves the look, feel and the usability. In addition the content creators find it easy to use.

Anything else you want us to know about SubjectsPlus or your process of switching to SubjectsPlus?

If you are person who implements SubjectsPlus, you must have a good knowledge of HTML and CSS. You must know some basic PHP and know how to administer a MySQL database. These skills are used for customization and installation. Except for the server setup, I have done most things myself. Any 'webby/techie' could do this.

However, if you are not a techie librarian but have a designated programmer set up the system, the web admin interface is sufficient for most administrative tasks. If you are the only content provider or librarian making a guide, it is very easy to use SubjectsPlus (you need no programming, HTML and so on.)

Learn more

See SubjectsPlus in action at Middlebury at *http://www.middlebury.edu/academics/lib/research/db-subject*.

SubjectsPlus was developed by the Ithaca College Library as a way to allow librarians to organize and present their data to patrons easily (see Figure 10.1). It allows for the storage of subject guides, A–Z lists and lists of staff members with their specialties. All of this is then published to the web, making it

Figure 10.1 Computer science research guide at Ithaca College Library

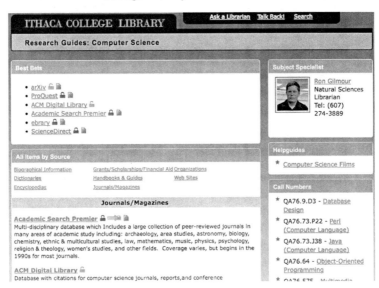

easier to research a specific topic, such as computer science (*http://www.ithacalibrary.com/sp/subjects/cs*).

One problem with managing static HTML pages is that you often want links to appear on more than one page, but that means you have multiple places to look when making updates. SubjectsPlus enables you to add a resource to the system just once and then have it appear on multiple guides. SubjectsPlus also has you associate an 'expert' with each subject guide, so patrons know whom to contact at the library or on campus should they have additional questions about the topic they are researching.

Library à la Carte™, from the Oregon State University Library, is another alternative to using static HTML pages for your subject guides. Like SubjectsPlus, it allows for the easy creation of dynamic subject guides. Unlike SubjectsPlus, Library à la Carte™ does not handle your A–Z lists and staff directories, but it does allow you to create course pages and tutorials.

10.2 Open source in the real world: Library à la Carte™

Kim Griggs, Programmer Analyst, Margaret Mellinger, Science Librarian, and Jane Nichols, Social Sciences/ Humanities Librarian
Oregon State University Libraries
Corvallis OR, USA

Why did you decide to use Library à la Carte™ in your library?

At the time that we developed Library à la Carte™, there were only a few software products available for the creation of library course and subject web pages. We assessed those that were available and didn't feel that they matched our need to add Web 2.0 functionality to the guides as we desired. LibGuides hadn't yet come out. Thus, we turned to developing an in-house solution.

How are you using Library à la Carte™ in your library?

Subject librarians are using it to create and manage course assignment pages and subject guides. Instruction librarians are using it to build tutorials.

How long have you been using Library à la Carte™ in your library?

Since its original iteration as the interactive course assignment pages (ICAP) tool in 2006/07.

What was the process of switching from proprietary to open source like?

Our previous practice was to create course and subject pages in html using Dreamweaver and Contribute templates. The process of switching was mostly a matter of understanding how a web content management system functions differently from using html templates. Training was needed for librarians to take advantage of all the features of Library à la Carte™. When librarians moved the content into Library à la Carte™, they had many more options for how to present that content.

What do you think of Library à la Carte™ now?

We like it and plan to continue to develop it. Our current focus is on using it for making tutorials and on hosting Library à la Carte™ through a cloud computing environment.

What do others in your library say about Library à la Carte™?

Responses are positive and librarians and library administrators are engaged in and supportive of its continued development.

Anything else you want us to know about Library à la Carte™ or your process of switching to Library à la Carte™?

The source code has been downloaded hundreds of times since its release in 2007. The tool is currently being used at over 20 libraries that we know about, including Reed College, Portland Community College, California State University (multiple campuses), University of Arizona, University of Montreal and Sheffield Hallam University.

Library à la Carte™ offers your staff an easy way to manage guides for their areas of expertise without having any knowledge of web design or development (see Figure 10.2). From the Library à la Carte™ administration area you can easily create your guide by clicking the link 'Create a New Subject Guide.' Your guide can then be made up of various tabs with information on each. As in SubjectsPlus, you need to choose an expert and include their information so that researchers can easily find the right person to direct their questions to. Once your page is created you click the 'Publish' button and your page is available on the library's site (see Figure 10.3).

Figure 10.2 The Library à la Carte™ administration area

Figure 10.3 A sample Library à la Carte™ subject guide on open source software

So, how do you choose between the two (and the many other alternatives available)? Try them out; both offer you the option to try a demo. See which one best meets your library's needs. As with many of the open source products mentioned in this book, SubjectsPlus (*http://groups.google .com/group/subjectsplus*) and Library à la Carte™ (*http://ala carte.library.oregonstate.edu/forum*) also offer online communities where users and developers can communicate with each other about problems, suggested uses and future developments; use them to assist in your decision making process. As stated before, the process of choosing an open source application is no different from that of choosing a proprietary option; you must research and try the products before making a final decision.

Additional research tools

Having a dynamic way to manage subject guides is just the first step in providing better services to our patrons; we also have many other research tools in our library that we would like to make accessible to our patrons via our websites. reSearcher (*http://researcher.sfu.ca*) is a suite of tools to do just that.

10.3 Open source in the real world: reSearcher

Dan Hoyte, Senior Library Systems Technician
Chapman University Leatherby Libraries
Orange CA, USA

Why did you decide to use reSearcher in your library?

Several factors went into the decision. Primary was the fact that we wanted finer control over the data that drove our link resolver. Secondary was the need to implement an ERM. We were able to accomplish those goals and save the university over 60 per cent of the cost of our previous solution.

How are you using reSearcher in your library?

We are currently utilizing the link resolving (GODOT), knowledge base (CUFTS) and electronic resource management. We are in the process of implementing federated searching (DbWiz). Our production system is run by Simon Fraser University, Canada. We also maintain a local backup and testing server locally.

How long have you been using reSearcher in your library?

We have been using reSearcher for nearly three years.

Did you have any trouble implementing reSearcher in your library?

We found setting up reSearcher was actually easier than setting up some of the proprietary packages that we tested.

137

What was the process of switching from proprietary to open source like?

The data that we had to move from our proprietary system into reSearcher was simply reformatted and uploaded to reSearcher. The most difficult part of the process was shifting the attitudes of library management to allow us to use open source. The technical side went smoothly.

Did you have any help installing, migrating to, or setting up reSearcher?

Other than having the networking group set up our firewall, we did the entire implementation within the library (local server).

What do you think of reSearcher now?

The more that we use reSearcher, the more we like it. It was amazing how well it fitted our needs. Since we have been able to help steer some of the development it is even more in tune with the way that we work.

What do others in your library say about reSearcher?

They are most impressed with the way that reSearcher answered the difficulties that we were experiencing with our previous system. They are pleased with the control that we now have over our data.

Anything else you want us to know about reSearcher or your process of switching to reSearcher?

Just that we are well pleased with the choice to go with reSearcher. We are looking forward to moving to our own server, in the next couple of years.

Learn more

See reSearcher in action at Chapman University at *http://cufts2.lib.sfu.ca/CRDB/COU*.

reSearcher was developed by the Simon Fraser University Library to help lower the barrier of entry into the electronic resource management arena for small and poor libraries. The tools provided in the reSearcher suite enable libraries to provide their patrons with streamlined access to electronic resources without the usual license fees associated with such services.

Included in reSearcher is CUFTS (*http://researcher.sfu.ca/cufts*) for serials management; GODOT (*http://researcher.sfu.ca/godot*), a link resolver; dbWiz (*http://researcher.sfu.ca/dbwiz*) for federated searching; and Open Knowledgebase (*http://researcher.sfu.ca/openkb*) to manage an open database of journal titles and publishers to be used within CUFTS (see Figure 10.4).

Each of the tools included in the reSearcher suite is meant to work in conjunction with the others to provide a better

Figure 10.4 The CUFTS page for technology and operations management[2] at the Simon Fraser University Library

service to all involved. Kevin Stranack writes in his amazing overview of the reSearcher suite:

> From its earliest days, *reSearcher* and its predecessors relied upon the cooperative spirit of libraries, their innovation and leadership, and their willingness to pool their limited resources, both in terms of staff and money, to create better technologies and services for their clients. The collaborative spirit of *reSearcher* continues today, with the ongoing support provided by the two major library consortia, COPPUL and BCELN, and the willingness of individual libraries to provide startup funding for new initiatives that will enhance the project and ultimately benefit the wider library community. *reSearcher* is an important example of the value of both open source and library collaboration.[3]

To learn more about the suite and how each module interacts with the others, I highly recommend you to read Kevin's article and some of the others listed on the official reSearcher site (*http://researcher.sfu.ca/documents*).

Online course management

As more and more educational materials become available online, libraries need to start thinking of new models for educating patrons about library use, new technologies, research practices and many other topics. In tough times we see that people are more likely to turn to their libraries for free access to the internet, free access to job search materials and free access to workshops.[4] At the same time, libraries are suffering from the same economic woes, so providing additional free services can be difficult.

One way to offer our patrons an added benefit without too much of an investment, and without the need for providing more space in the library, is to start to offer online workshops. Moodle (*http://www.moodle.org*) is an open source course management system, which can be used to help manage your course materials, online lectures, research references and plenty more.

10.4 Open source in the real world: Moodle

Georgia Katsarou, Librarian
International Center for Hellenic and Mediterranean Studies, and College Year in Athens Library
Athens, Greece

Why did you decide to use Moodle in your library?

We wanted to use a course management system in order to offer more up-to-date teaching facilities to our faculty and in order to facilitate the communication between faculty and students. Our IT support suggested Moodle because they were familiar with it and knew that it is working well and can fit our needs.

How are you using Moodle in your library?

We are the administrators and in brief we create new courses, update data, add and remove resources, create and delete user accounts, assign roles for the users and train faculty on how to use it.

How long have you been using Moodle in your library?

Two years.

Did you have any trouble implementing Moodle in your library?

No.

Did you have any help installing, migrating to, or setting up Moodle?

Our IT support did the installation. There was no need for data migration since we didn't have a course management system before.

I did the settings and asked for the IT department's help just once when I wanted them to increase the file upload size limit. It was very easy to use and understand and the available documentation is clear and comprehensive.

What do you think of Moodle now?

I think it's a very good and usable software with useful and user friendly features. Up to now we had no problems at all and I was surprised that we didn't encounter any problems due to bugs. I would definitely recommend it to other possible users.

What do others in your library say about Moodle?

Everybody seems to be happy about it. It is significant that they don't have to spend a lot of time in order to learn how to use it.

Anything else you want us to know about Moodle or your process of switching to Moodle?

As is the case with any open source application, the administrators have to read the documentation thoroughly.

Using Moodle, librarians can create classes on topics related to their community and provide online access to the information (see Figure 10.5), for example they could give a series of workshops on real estate in hard times. A librarian could offer the workshops in person at the library and online simultaneously, or completely online (so there was no need for the library to provide a large public meeting space).

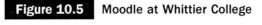

Figure 10.5 Moodle at Whittier College

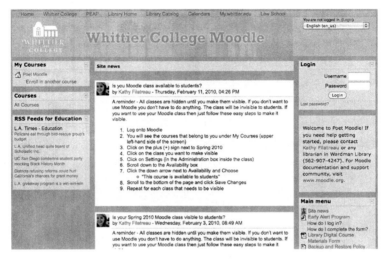

Moodle offers the ability for instructors to upload materials, links and course schedules so that students can work in their own time. It also makes it easy for students to communicate with each other and the instructor using chat rooms and message boards. All of these services are found in popular proprietary offerings, but without the added license fees or use restrictions. This means that libraries can offer additional services to their patrons without having to go outside their allotted budget.

Teaching our patrons

Using any one (or combination) of the tools listed in this chapter, your library can offer patrons easier access to information, and these tools not only benefit our patrons, but also make our jobs more efficient simply by putting the right tool for the job in our hands. Next time you are updating your library's subject guide with your HTML editor, think about using a tool meant just for that purpose, and instead of printing out handouts for your newest workshop, why not store the information online for easy access and printing by the attendees themselves?

In libraries we often get stuck in a rut. We continue to do things the way we always have because we don't know of any better option. Well now you know about four open source tools that will assist in providing information to and teaching our patrons.

Notes

1. To learn more about the research links project at Jenkins Law Library you can read my article 'Following the Yellow Brick Road to Simplified Link Management' at *http://www.web2 learning.net/publications-presentations/following-the-yellow-brick-road-to-simplified-link-management.*
2. See *http://cufts2.lib.sfu.ca/CRDB/BVAS/browse/facets/subject/594.*
3. Stranack, Kevin. 'The reSearcher Software Suite: a case study of library collaboration and open source software development.' *Serials Librarian 55,* no. 1/2 (2008): 117–139.
4. Rettig, Jim. 'Libraries Stand Ready to Help in Tough Economic Times.' *The Huffington Post,* December 11, 2008. *http://www.huffingtonpost.com/jim-rettig/libraries-stand-ready-to_b_150268.html.*

Open source library automation

I remember when my library first introduced the automated catalog. It was a black screen computer with bright green lettering. It was amazing to me that I could now search for the books I wanted without having to finger through the card catalog. We have come a long way since then and have many choices available to us. One of the choices that has recently become more viable is the open source integrated library system.

Open source faces

One obvious way to provide your patrons with better services is to improve the look, feel and functionality of your OPAC (online public access catalog). Although there are proprietary applications to do this, they can be very costly, making your overall library automation budget stretch its limits. An alternative would be to use one of the many open source OPAC layers available for download today without any extra cost to you or your library.

Scriblio

The first major open source OPAC to hit the web was WPopac, now known as Scriblio (*http://scriblio.net*), which was developed by Casey Bisson while at the Lamson Library at the Plymouth State University in 2006.[1] Scriblio takes the power of the WordPress content management system and integrates the OPAC into it. Libraries using Scriblio simply use WordPress to design their entire library site and then patrons can search for books from the library homepage (see Figure 11.1) without ever realizing that they have left the library site for the OPAC.

11.1 Open source in the real world: Scriblio

Brett Bonfield, Director
Collingswood Public Library
Collingswood NJ, USA

Why did you decide to use Scriblio in your library?

For me, the initial decision to use Scriblio and the ongoing decision to stick with it are both difficult and obvious. I really like using WordPress and know it well – I created a very basic Scriblio site even before I had my first interview for my current job, and setting it up took just a few hours – and I really like Casey Bisson as a person and as a web developer: our visions for libraries are awfully similar. For instance, Scriblio creates unified websites: for Scriblio libraries, the catalog and the rest of the website look alike and run on exactly the same software. What closed the deal for us was Scriblio's ability to pull in funding and its decision to turn some of that funding into free hosting for CollingswoodLib.org (and similar libraries).

How are you using Scriblio in your library?

As our website.

How long have you been using Scriblio in your library?

The website has been live for almost a year, though I started working with Scriblio (and with Casey Bisson, its developer) about 18 months ago.

Did you have any trouble implementing Scriblio in your library?

There have been issues, sure. Many of them have been fixed, but there are a few outstanding issues.

What was the process of switching from proprietary to open source like?

We didn't really switch. Millennium is still there, including its web OPAC interface. Scriblio just complements it.

Did you have any help installing, migrating to, or setting up Scriblio?

I worked directly with Casey Bisson, the main developer.

What do you think of Scriblio now?

I like it. Scriblio isn't perfect, but I'm very comfortable with it and excited about where it's heading. While I'll be happier when there's a larger developer community, more internal interest in standards, and better documentation, I have the ability to help make these changes.

What do others in your library say about Scriblio?

Many people like it; some prefer the old system. It's like Dewey: most of the people who have gotten to know it well have developed a fondness for it. The rest of the world wants a website that works like Google and a shelving system that works like Barnes & Noble.

Anything else you want us to know about Scriblio or your process of switching to Scriblio?

I have written a full article about my decision here: *http://www.inthelibrarywiththeleadpipe.org/2009/ w-e-b-s-i-t-e-find-out-what-it-means-to-me/.*

Figure 11.1 Scriblio at the Collingswood Public Library

VuFind

The second open source OPAC release was in 2007 with VuFind (*http://www.vufind.org*). Released by Villanova University to 'empower users by supporting personalization and social networking services such as tagging and peer-to-peer comment sharing,'[2] VuFind's simple interface quickly became very popular among OPAC critics (see Figure 11.2).

Blacklight

Shortly after the release of VuFind came Blacklight (*http://rubyforge.org/projects/blacklight/*). Released in 2008,[3]

Figure 11.2 VuFind at the Falvey Memorial Library at Villanova University

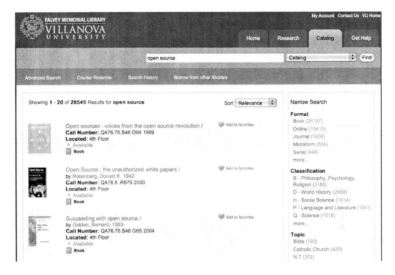

11.2 Open source in the real world: VuFind

Joel Harbottle

LCG Library

South Launceston, Australia

Why did you decide to use VuFind in your library?

We decided to use VuFind in our library because we found it was an easier interface for our patrons to navigate and understand compared to the OPAC packaged with our LMS.

How are you using VuFind in your library?

VuFind is used as our primary OPAC and we also give our patrons the option to use the original OPAC, which was packaged with our LMS.

How long have you been using VuFind in your library?

We started to look at VuFind as another option to our existing OPAC during January 2008. We decided we would use VuFind as an alternative OPAC on the 20th January 2008 (two weeks later); during early February 2008 we installed VuFind and connected to our LMS's training database, and we asked some patrons to conduct some searches in VuFind and give us their feedback on its interface and how easy it is to use. With positive feedback we installed VuFind onto a production server and went live with it on the 1st March 2008. (We use VuFind as our primary OPAC, but still offer our patrons the option to use the OPAC which was packaged with our LMS.)

VuFind has now been in use in our library for over one and a half years.

Did you have any trouble implementing VuFind in your library?

No, we didn't have any trouble at all implementing VuFind in our library. It was all quite straightforward and we didn't have any problems. The major part was to make some minor changes to our LMS.

What was the process of switching from proprietary to open source like?

We didn't have much of a process in switching over to VuFind. As our LMS isn't a proprietary system, we use Evergreen, which is an open source ILS. Our main concern during the process of switching was our clients and how they would find the new OPAC, but we found we didn't have to worry, because our patrons found VuFind easier to navigate than our existing OPAC and really like the interface. Our patrons gave us loads of feedback, which helps us identify things we could improve on, and they continue to do so today.

Did you have any help installing, migrating to, or setting up VuFind?

No, we didn't have much help installing, migrating to, or setting up VuFind. But we did refer to the VuFind website quite a bit if we didn't understand a particular part during the process.

What do you think of VuFind now?

Today, VuFind blows us away with its fantastic interface and wonderful ease of use, just as it did when I first started looking at it at the beginning of 2008.

What do others in your library say about VuFind?

We are constantly getting great feedback about VuFind and its ease of use from our library's patrons.

Anything else you want us to know about VuFind or your process of switching to VuFind?

I would highly recommend VuFind to any library looking at a new OPAC; it is a truly wonderful Web 2.0 OPAC.

Blacklight is a project to improve the library's services by upgrading the library's OPAC. Blacklight sits on top of your existing integrated library system and presents your data to patrons in an easy to understand, visually appealing interface (see Figure 11.3).

Figure 11.3 Blacklight at the University of Virginia Library

11.3 Open source in the real world: Blacklight

Tom Cramer, Associate Director Digital Library Systems & Services
Stanford University Libraries and Academic Information Resources
Stanford CA, USA

Why did you decide to use Blacklight in your library?

We chose Blacklight for a number of reasons.

1. *Technology strategy and maintainability*. Stanford University Libraries made a strategic choice to embrace Ruby on Rails (RoR) as its end-user facing application development language at the end of 2008. So far, our experience with RoR and Blacklight has been consistent with our expectations. We have trained a half dozen developers with no previous RoR experience to become competent developers in well under a month, and test coverage of Blacklight exceeds 70 per cent of its code base.

2. *Architecture, functions and feature set*. Blacklight has demonstrated support for three key features that we think are critical for a next generation search application. These are support for non-MARC data, object-specific behaviors and tailored views.

3. *Community*. Blacklight has a solid core of institutions and expert individuals committed to, and contributing to, its code base. Very early on, the principal stakeholders in the project at the University of Virginia demonstrated that they were open and eager to take code contributions, ideas and support (in many forms) from other institutions and individuals. This encouraged us to adopt Blacklight ourselves, and gave us the confidence that if we adopted it, we would have a chance to help further a common

code base, and not have to take on long-term support for all our local modifications and enhancements.

How are you using Blacklight in your library?

We are currently using Blacklight as:

- a next generation catalog (see *http://searchworks .stanford.edu*)
- a front end for various Fedora repositories
- a search, browse and view interface for specialized digital library applications (for example, digitized medieval manuscripts).

How long have you been using Blacklight in your library?

We formally adopted Blacklight in December 2008.

Did you have any trouble implementing Blacklight in your library?

We spent the first two to three quarters after adopting Blacklight working with its core team of committers to refactor the codebase, making it more portable, better tested and more feature rich. This work culminated in the Blacklight 2.0 release in spring 2009. After this work, we have found implementing new instances of Blacklight is a straightforward task. The most demanding task in setting up a Blacklight instance is in designing and populating the underlying solr index.

What was the process of switching from proprietary to open source like?

We have had other experiences in adopting open source software, which were key factors in weighing Blacklight's community, architecture and maintainability so heavily in deciding to adopt it. After paying the upfront cost of adopting a new technology (RoR) and a new application (Blacklight), we've found it liberating to work on an open code base. Our librarians have made some extremely particular requests for how data and functionality should work in the new system, and being able to manipulate the underlying data and the application to our requirements is an extremely satisfying experience, especially compared to working with most proprietary systems.

Did you have any help installing, migrating to, or setting up Blacklight?

We have found the Blacklight developers list to be the best resource for technical support (and we've received much from its contributors).

What do you think of Blacklight now?

It's an excellent tool, and one of the centerpieces to our digital library strategy.

What do others in your library say about Blacklight?

They appreciate its feature set and flexibility, and are eager for more functions and data types to be added as quickly as possible.

Learn more:

See *http://searchworks.stanford.edu*.

Of particular note are:

- the advanced search feature (developed at Stanford, and soon to be checked into the common codebase), available at *http://searchworks .stanford.edu/advanced*
- the browse nearby a call number feature
- the real time availability display, showing location and status for all items at a glance on the search results page.

SOPAC2

Finally came the release of SOPAC2 (*http://thesocialopac.net*) by John Blyberg and the Darien Library later in 2008.[4] SOPAC2 went one step further than the previous two options and followed the Scriblio model by integrating the OPAC directly into a content management system, the difference being that SOPAC2 is integrated into Drupal instead of WordPress. This means that the library can now have a seamless look and feel, and patrons can search through both the library site and the OPAC (see Figure 11.4).

Choosing an OPAC

There are four free open source OPACs for you to choose from, so how to make the choice? Part of your decision is going to be personal preference because they each offer very similar services to each other. The other part, and this is a big one, is to determine whether or not the OPAC has connectors for your particular integrated library system yet. If the OPAC cannot communicate with it then it's not the

Figure 11.4 SOPAC2 at the Darien Library

11.4 Open source in the real world: SOPAC

John Blyberg, Assistant Director for Innovation and User
Experience
Darien Library
Darien CT, USA

Why did you decide to use SOPAC in your library?

No product on the market exists to meet the requirements
of our digital strategy, which is to unify all of our electronic
resources into a single, interactive portal.

How are you using SOPAC in your library?

We are using it as a complete OPAC replacement and as
an additional online service to our users. Out staff also
use it for collection development, information services
and readers advisory.

How long have you been using SOPAC in your library?

Since September 2008.

**What was the process of switching from proprietary to
open source like?**

Very easy.

What do you think of SOPAC now?

We love it!

What do others in your library say about SOPAC?

They love it!

---

one for you. That said, there are always new developments
happening and so if you like one more than another, just
contact the developers and see what it would take to get a
connector written for your integrated library system.

All four offer an efficient, easy to understand search box.
Although we as librarians prefer to perform more complex

searches, the average internet user is a fan of the Google model, also known as keyword searching. All of these tools take that into account. In fact, Scriblio and Blacklight only offer a single search box option, so there is no advanced search.[5] SOPAC2 offers a slightly more advanced search page and VuFind offers a traditional-looking library advanced search page. Although the search systems are all different, they all offer the option to filter your results by various different headings and item types, making it easy to narrow your results down to the right subset of items.

In addition to the simple search interfaces, all of these options offer permanent links to bibliographic records and search results. This means that as a librarian you can copy the URL from the address bar in your browser and send it to a patron via email or instant message and when the patron clicks the link it will take them to the same screen you were looking at. This is something that is slowly becoming standard in the traditional OPAC, but is not yet widespread.

All of these options also take into account modern social web features such as RSS feeds and commenting. VuFind and SOPAC2 go a step further and allow for patrons to add tags. SOPAC2 also allows patrons to add ratings and reviews to records in the catalog. All of this extra data is then stored outside the integrated library system so as not to interfere with librarian-supplied data, while still giving the patrons a sense of belonging to the library in more ways than one.

Open source it all

If your library is planning to change the integrated library system experience for the entire library, not just patrons, then maybe an open source integrated library system is the right choice for you. There are currently two major possibilities on the market: Koha (*http://koha-community.org*) and Evergreen (*http://open-ils.org*). In addition to these two there many other small projects that are worth looking at as well.

Koha

Development on Koha[6] started in 1999 in New Zealand. Members of the Horowhenua Library Trust (*http://www .library.org.nz*) in New Zealand decided that after contracting development of the integrated library system to Katipo Communications they wanted the code released into the wild for use by any and all libraries worldwide. In January 2000, the first version of Koha was released.[7] Ten years later, the system is being used by at least 945 libraries worldwide.[8]

11.5 Open source in the real world: Koha

Owen Leonard, Web Developer
Nelsonville Public Library
Nelsonville OH, USA

Why did you decide to use Koha in your library?

We first started investigating open source library systems when we began to have some concerns about the ILS we were using at the time. We were disappointed with the quality of support we were receiving. We were interested in upgrading that system, but we were told that to do so we would have to spend thousands of dollars on new hardware.

At the same time we were interested in providing additional services to the public via the OPAC and using the data in the database. Unfortunately, we didn't have easy access to either one: there was no option for customizing the content or appearance of the OPAC, and there was no way to connect to the system's database using common tools like MySQL.

At the time Koha was the most mature open source ILS available and the community surrounding it was active and helpful. When we looked at the list of services any system would have to match in order for us to be able to switch to it Koha didn't match everything, but we knew that we had the power to make it into what we wanted.

How are you using Koha in your library?

We use just about all of Koha's functionality with a few exceptions: acquisitions, serials and original cataloging. Historically acquisitions and serials management were not elements of our previous commercial ILSes that we paid for, so our workflow when moving to Koha didn't include those aspects. However, as serials management improves in Koha it's becoming more and more attractive as a viable solution for us.

How long have you been using Koha in your library?

We went live with Koha on September 2, 2003.

Did you have any trouble implementing Koha in your library?

Whatever 'trouble' we had implementing Koha we faced with the full understanding of the task before us. When we made the decision to move to Koha the software hadn't yet reached version 2.0. We knew that we would have to sponsor the addition of MARC support before we could make the switch. We knew that we'd be doing some data imports by hand, and that we'd be fixing bugs.

What was the process of switching from proprietary to open source like?

The process of switching from a proprietary vendor confirmed for us that switching to open source was the right decision. The software we were using at the time did not make it easy for us to export our data. When it came time to export some of our data we tried to use a tool we found in our system, but it didn't work. We contacted the vendor and asked why it was broken and they told us, 'You have pay us to turn that on.'

Did you have any help installing, migrating to, or setting up Koha?

We did everything with in-house staff, with the frequent support of the Koha mailing list and IRC channel.

What do you think of Koha now?

Koha continues to work very well for us. We really enjoy the flexibility of having direct access to our database for performing custom reports. It's empowering to be able to find a bug, diagnose it, develop a fix, and submit it for inclusion in the next version. I love that we can feature our own content on the OPAC and customize it to match our website.

What do others in your library say about Koha?

Being Koha users has taught many of the staff that we have the power to make changes to our own software. Staff will report bugs to me and help to diagnose problems knowing that we can actually make a difference. This is a big change from the mindset of living under a proprietary vendor and fearing that bug reports will never be heard about again.

Anything else you want us to know about Koha or your process of switching to Koha?

Our original migration from a proprietary vendor's system to Koha is completely atypical: we were the first Koha public library in the United States, and we went through a lot to make it work. I think that work has helped pave the way for the process to be easier for libraries adopting Koha today. Improvements in the software and the arrival on the scene of Koha hosting and support companies make the prospect of moving to Koha no different, in terms of effort, than moving to any other ILS.

What we learned this year was that having moved to Koha, we're in a much better position to be able to pick and choose the paid support we want. Now that there are

> choices in the Koha support market, libraries that use Koha are no longer tied down to one vendor for support and development. That makes a huge difference to a library that is unhappy with their vendor. With a proprietary ILS, a change in vendor is a change in ILS requiring a full-blown migration. If you're using Koha and you're not getting the support you want you have the option of choosing another support company. It's incredibly empowering to know that you have that choice.

Unlike many traditional library systems, Koha is completely web-based; this means that staff functionalities and the OPAC are accessed through your browser. In its current version, 3.2, Koha offers access to all of the major modules necessary to run a library: patron management, cataloging, circulation, acquisitions and serials (see Figure 11.5). There are also many tools and reports available to automate processes and provide statistical data.

Like many of the open source OPACs, Koha offers patrons social functionality as part of its standard OPAC. These include things like RSS feeds, commenting, tagging and creating lists of favorites in the library (see Figure 11.6).

Figure 11.5 Koha's web-based staff client

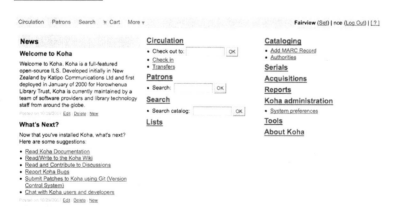

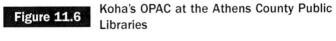

Figure 11.6 Koha's OPAC at the Athens County Public Libraries

Also like the open source OPACs, Koha provides patrons and librarians with permanent links to bibliographic records and search result screens, making reference work just that little bit easier.

Evergreen

Although six years younger than Koha, Evergreen is a strong open source integrated library system contender on the market today. Evergreen was developed by the PINES library system (*http://gapines.org*) in Georgia, USA, and was debuted on September 5, 2006.[9] Evergreen was different from any open source system before. It was originally designed to manage the 252 libraries in the PINES consortium, making it the biggest open source release the library world had seen to date.

Since that initial release, Evergreen has been adopted by at least 544[10] libraries worldwide. In its current version, 1.6, Evergreen offers libraries access to many of the modules they will need to run their library: patron management, cataloging and circulation (see Figure 11.7). There are also reports and tools to help libraries automate process and

11.6 Open source in the real world: Evergreen

Karen Collier, Public Services Librarian, and Andrea Buntz
Neiman, Technical Services Librarian
Kent County Public Library
Chestertown MD, USA

Why did you decide to use Evergreen in your library?

For our new ILS we were looking for a certain combination of price, features and support. Evergreen had the features we wanted at an excellent price, with top notch support available. The freedom and opportunity for community involvement that come with open source software were icing on the cake.

How are you using Evergreen in your library?

Evergreen is our integrated library system, providing circulation, cataloging and reporting functionality, as well as our public access catalog.

How long have you been using Evergreen in your library?

We've been running Evergreen live since June 4, 2008.

Did you have any trouble implementing Evergreen in your library?

Migrating to Evergreen turned out to be significantly less trouble than we thought it might be. We've heard our share of migration horror stories, but ours was painless. We were running Horizon on Tuesday and Evergreen on Wednesday with no interruption to services.

What was the process of switching from proprietary to open source like?

The move to open source has been an eye opening experience. The community of Evergreen developers, users and enthusiasts has proven active, helpful and welcoming. And the freedom that comes with open source is like a breath of fresh air.

Did you have any help installing, migrating to, or setting up?

Alpha-G Consulting (*http://www.alphagconsulting.com*) performed our migration from Horizon to Evergreen, and Equinox Software (*http://esilibrary.com*) provides ongoing hosting and support for us.

What do you think of Evergreen now?

We love Evergreen. We could not be happier with our decision.

What do others in your library say about Evergreen?

Seniors love the single search box in the Basic Search interface – simple to use! Teens love the single search box – because it's Google-like! All patrons like the ability to manage their account and their holds online.

Anything else you want us to know about Evergreen or your process of switching to Evergreen?

We believe that open source and public libraries share a lot of common values and goals, among those freedom of information, equal and open access, and community-oriented practices. We are happy to support open source in public libraries, and we will continue to urge other public libraries to make the same choice.

gather data. Although it does not yet offer an acquisitions or serials module,[11] these modules are in development and should be available in a future release of Evergreen.

Evergreen's OPAC also provides patrons with a clean look and feel they have come to expect from modern websites (see Figure 11.8). The Evergreen OPAC allows patrons to narrow their searches using facets (also known as authorized headings), browse for items on the shelf around the title they are viewing, share items with fellow patrons by creating 'book bags,' and copy and paste any URL into emails and websites.

Figure 11.7 Circulation and cataloguing in the Evergreen staff client

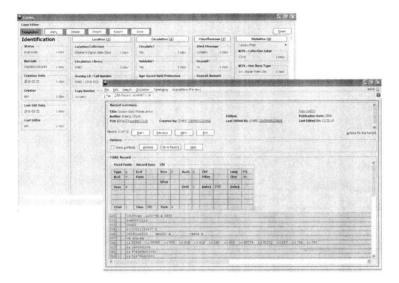

Figure 11.8 The Evergreen OPAC at Kent County Public Library

Similarities and differences

Both OPACs also offer enhanced content from outside services. This means that they make use of book jackets and reviews from sites like Amazon.com, Google Books (*http://books .google.com*) and LibraryThing (*http://librarything.com*). These added services make the OPAC a little bit more appealing to patrons as they browse your collection.

Like the four open source OPACs, Koha and Evergreen are similar in many ways, and different in a few. Evergreen was developed with the consortium in mind, so although Koha can and does work in a consortium environment, Evergreen handles the consortium rules and permissions much better. On the flip side, Koha makes more sense for large and/or special libraries because it has the ability to manage your library's acquisitions and serials. That said, these small differences are slowly disappearing as Evergreen developers work on finishing serials and acquisitions support and Koha developers work on creating system groups and consortium-like permissions.

The beauty of the open source integrated library system is that the more libraries that are using the system the more new and improved features become available. When Koha was developed it was made for one library and its specific needs. When Evergreen was developed it was meant to work in one specific library consortium environment. Over the years both systems have been adopted by libraries that are unlike the original audience and the developments that have come out of those adoptions makes both tools more powerful and valuable.

As with any open source application, it is important to test all the systems available to you before making a decision. Both Evergreen and Koha offer online public demos (usually in more than one place) that you can try before you decide. Once your decision is made you can handle the migration on your own or turn to any number of support companies worldwide.[12]

Taking the leap

Deciding to change such a fundamental part of your library's operations as the integrated library system or OPAC can be scary and, like choosing any of the applications in this book, might not be the right step for your library. It is important to look at open source alternatives alongside your traditional resources so that you can make an educated decision about your automation needs. As with any software decision, be sure to consult your colleagues worldwide to see what their experiences have been and what they recommend.

Notes

1. Bisson, Casey. 'Designing an OPAC for Web 2.0' presented at the ALA Midwinter, January 20, 2006. *http://homepage .mac.com/misterbisson/Presentations/ALAMidwinter-2006Jan20.pdf.*
2. Lucia, Joe. 'Villanova University Releases VUFIND, an Open Source Next Generation Library Catalog.' *Library Technology Guides*, July 15, 2007. *http://www.librarytechnology .org/ltg-displaytext.pl?RC=12664.*
3. Sadler, Bess. 'First Release!.' *RubyForge: Blacklight*, January 26, 2008. *http://rubyforge.org/forum/forum.php?forum_id=21035.*
4. Blyberg, John. 'SOPAC 2 Released: the socialopac.net launched.' *blyberg.net*, September 25, 2008. *http://www .blyberg.net/2008/09/25/sopac-2-released-thesocialopacnet-launched/.*
5. At the time of writing, Stanford University has developed an advanced search module for Blacklight, but it has not yet been added to the codebase for all to benefit from.
6. Koha is the Maori word for gift, but not just any kind of gift; it is a gift that is offered with an expectation that it will be reciprocated.
7. Eyler, Pat. 'Koha: a gift to libraries from New Zealand.' *Linux Journal* 106 (2003): 1.
8. This number was found by searching for libraries using Koha on lib-web-cats (*http://www.librarytechnology.org/libwebcats/*). It is important to note that since anyone can download the software and use it without charge, there is no way to know for sure how many libraries might be using Koha.

9. 'Georgia's 252 PINES Public Libraries Preparing Debut of Evergreen Software, Web-based Catalog.' *Library Technology Guides*, August 21, 2006. *http://www.librarytechnology.org/ltg-displaytext.pl?RC=12162*.

10. This number was found by searching for libraries using Evergreen on lib-web-cats (*http://www.librarytechnology.org/libwebcats/*). It is important to note that since anyone can download the software and use it without charge, there is no way to know for sure how many libraries might be using Evergreen.

11. As of May 1, 2010, there are versions of acquisitions and serials modules available for testing. To learn more about acquisitions you can read my summary from the 2010 Evergreen conference at *http://www.web2learning.net/archives/3770*; Ian Walls has a nice summary of serials also from the conference, at *http://bywatersolutions.com/?p=474*.

12. Eric Lease Morgan has compiled a list of open source support companies that have been known to work with libraries in the past at *http://infomotions.com/tmp/oss/support.html*. As he notes, this list is not exhaustive, but it's a great place to start your research.

Afterword

As with many other books on library technology, I know that all of this information can make one's head spin. There are so many things to learn about open source software, from its history to its software uses, but it is important to keep at least these few things in mind when deciding to adopt open source software.

Open source is about more than the software; it is about the community around the software. If you decide to use open source software in your library, make an effort to participate in the community to show your support and to further the application.

As with all open source software, you want to keep in mind that just because a feature you need is not available at this time, it can easily be added by you or someone hired by you. Do not let the lack of a feature scare you out of using an open source library system; simply contact the development community and see if maybe there is a new feature in the works, or if you can submit some code to add the feature yourself.

Remember, 'free as in freedom.' With open source software you have the freedom to participate in, collaborate with, share with, develop for, move forward, change and improve the software you are using. Don't forget those basic freedoms when using open source in your library.

The library world is full of accounts of successes and failures of open source adoption; learn from them all. Use this guide as a jumping off point; always remember to talk to your colleagues and see what they've done, are doing and what they've experienced. Also be aware that there is much more out there that was not included in this book. If you don't like a suggestion that I have given, there are probably other alternatives that will meet your library's specific needs.

Finally, remember to help educate our fellow librarians about the true nature of open source. We cannot move forward and succeed if our colleagues are out there spreading the fear, uncertainty and doubt (FUD) that they have learned from those around them.

Appendix 1 Survey results

A total of 977 people from all over the world answered the survey. Table A1 shows the raw results used throughout this book (with only minor spelling corrections); you will note that not every question was answered by everyone.

Each question offered a field for further clarification; however, for the sake of space, not all full text answers are provided in this appendix. For complete full text results from the survey please refer to the official book website at *http://opensource.web2learning.net*.

Table A1   Types of library respondents worked in

What type of library do you work in?	Total	%
Academic library	395	42.93
Special library	116	12.61
Large public library	63	6.85
Medium public library	138	15.00
Small public library	80	8.70
One person library	10	1.09
School library	6	0.65
I'm a student	16	1.74
I'm unemployed at the moment	5	0.54
I don't work in a library (but I do work with libraries)	62	6.74
Other	29	3.15
Grand total	920	

Figure A1   Types of library respondents worked in

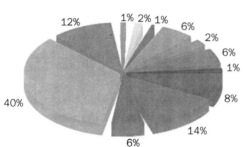

- Small Public Library (80)
- Medium Public Library (138)
- Large Public Library (63)
- Academic Library (393)
- Special Library (115)
- One Person Library (10)
- I'm a Student (16)
- I'm Unemployed at the moment (5)
- I don't work in a library (but I do work with libraries) (62)
- Other (24)
- No answer (57)
- Non completed (14)

Table A2   Countries respondents lived or worked in

What country do you live/work in?	Total	%
Argentina	5	0.55
Armenia	1	0.11
Australia	15	1.65
Austria	2	0.22
Barbados	1	0.11
Belarus	1	0.11
Belgium	4	0.44
Benin	1	0.11
Brazil	2	0.22
Canada	52	5.72
China	1	0.11
Croatia	2	0.22
Czech Republic	11	1.21
Denmark	5	0.55
Egypt	2	0.22
Estonia	1	0.11
Ethiopia	1	0.11
Finland	1	0.11
France	5	0.55
Georgia	1	0.11
Germany	34	3.74
Ghana	1	0.11
Greece	4	0.44

Table A2   Countries respondents lived or worked in (*Cont'd*)

What country do you live/work in?	Total	%
Hong Kong	2	0.22
Hungary	1	0.11
India	11	1.21
Indonesia	10	1.10
Iran	1	0.11
Ireland	4	0.44
Israel	1	0.11
Italy	3	0.33
Kalamazoo	1	0.11
Kenya	1	0.11
Kuwait	1	0.11
Malawi	4	0.44
México	2	0.22
Netherlands	4	0.44
Netherlands Antilles	1	0.11
New Zealand	9	0.99
Nigeria	1	0.11
Norway	2	0.22
Pakistan	3	0.33
Palestine	1	0.11
Poland	1	0.11
Portugal	4	0.44
Samoa	1	0.11
Singapore	3	0.33
South Africa	2	0.22
Spain	6	0.66
Sweden	3	0.33
Switzerland	5	0.55
Taiwan	1	0.11
Thailand	5	0.55
Turkey	2	0.22
United Kingdom	13	1.43
United States	645	70.96
Venezuela	1	0.11
Zimbabwe	1	0.11
Grand total	909	

Table A3   Types of department respondents worked in

What department do you work in? Check all that apply	Total	%
Reference	318	16.21
Cataloging	236	12.03
Acquisitions	171	8.72
Circulation	165	8.41
Serials	118	6.01
Information Technology	477	24.31
Development	138	7.03
Management	221	11.26
Training	16	0.82
Event Planning	76	3.87
None	26	1.33
Grand total	1962	

Figure A2   Types of department respondents worked in

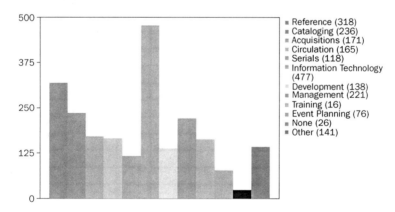

- Reference (318)
- Cataloging (236)
- Acquisitions (171)
- Circulation (165)
- Serials (118)
- Information Technology (477)
- Development (138)
- Management (221)
- Training (16)
- Event Planning (76)
- None (26)
- Other (141)

Table A4 How respondents completed the statement 'Open source is…'

Please complete the following sentence. Open source is...	Total	%
Insecure	36	3.68
Free of cost	356	36.44
Too hard to learn	47	4.81
Awesome	415	42.48
A fad	8	0.82
Risky	105	10.75
Unsupported	112	11.46
Poorly documented	139	14.23
Written by kids in their garage	18	1.84
Widely supported	281	28.76
Too new and unproven	39	3.99
Customizable	621	63.56
Community	527	53.94
Offers freedom	545	55.78
Proven	213	21.80
The way all programs started	79	8.09
All I'll use	64	6.55
Not worth my time	5	0.51
… I don't know	52	5.32
Peer reviewed	157	16.07
Used in several fields including business, science and academia	492	50.36
Other	129	13.20
Grand total	4440	

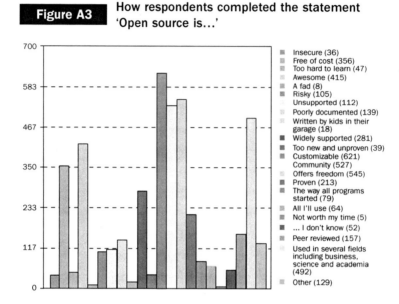

Figure A3 How respondents completed the statement 'Open source is...'

Of the 129 people who answered 'other,' 128 added other comments:

- full of hidden costs
- can be tricky to master
- a good deal for libraries
- amazing, but administration is too scared to use it
- first choice!
- great if you have on-site developers
- too new to risk trying
- a significant part of solving library issues
- more than likely not allowed by our campus IT
- these choices are way too imprecise
- all of the above

- mixed – each of the items on your list can apply to some and not others
- not widely enough used
- open standards and interoperability
- how I save my library money
- needs a good tech person on site familiar with open source
- very intriguing; I want to know more!
- rewarding
- all may occur since there are numerous projects
- very varied
- is all over the place and underpins many commercial technologies each application should be judged on its own individual merits within the context that you intend to use it
- total cost of ownership is not always apparent
- labor-intensive
- requires a little more skill/knowledge to set up and maintain
- sometimes harder to set up than commercial software
- freedom from library vendors
- hard for admin to accept
- a good resource
- often the only option; sometimes frustrating
- sometimes not available (or known) for apps my library needs
- still in its infancy
- can end up costing quite a bit in staff time
- offers an opportunity that sometimes is not available with vendor-based systems
- openly editable

- sexy
- frowned upon by corporate IT departments
- irregularly updated
- good alternative
- hard to convince IT and admin to use and support
- often used by people disdainful of 'noobs'
- hard to get training in
- a way to break out of the library systems lock-in paradigm
- expense is in the support and development
- requires more local support
- it varies with the s/w
- not quite there yet
- part of overall IT solutions
- innovative
- powerful
- correct
- riddled with hidden costs
- time consuming
- varied
- ethically correct
- misunderstood
- labor intensive
- requires initiative and consumes more of the user's time
- too broad a category to fit generalizations
- all of the above
- can't generalize
- a reasonable option in many cases

- often as good as, or better, than commercial equivalents
- global
- on the cutting edge
- not worse than commercial products
- preferable to proprietary technology where the community, governance and product are of a good quality
- is misunderstood
- good, but too few librarians know enough about what it is to want to use it
- depends on the product
- time consuming
- can help train IT outsiders in the field of your choice and act as a gateway for tech-savvy librarians to become programmers
- you can't generalize
- more reliable
- something we've looked into using
- should be more readily available!
- a tough sell to IT managers
- new but has potential!
- almost all I'll use
- while not 'free' is less costly than traditional software
- not all are usable and reliable
- more work to set up and maintain than vendor supplied software
- great in some instances and not so in other
- creative & responsive
- critical to success

- not as time-saving as you'd think
- widely misrepresented
- integrated library systems are not yet mature
- free like a puppy
- may be incompatible with existing system(s) and require special programming
- a lot of work
- highly variable: some is rock solid, some is not
- is less costly, although not free when local support is considered
- fine for those who have their own IT people to make it work
- secure
- time-consuming, useful, like keeping a pet
- excellent ROI
- underused
- requires troubleshooting
- an aid to being self-contained
- the way we want to go
- too costly in personnel
- often requires in-house expertise
- sometimes too confusing for the public
- reinventing the wheel
- patrons don't know how to use it
- profitable if you can leverage it
- an option to consider
- all of the above

- hit and miss
- the only way to move forward with a project when there is no software budget for it
- the only realistic option for me as I can't afford software otherwise, but I don't have funding to customize or obtain as much support as I would wish – but beggars can't be choosers and at least it makes my service viable!
- has great potential if properly supported by a strong community of users and developers
- over rated
- not allowed in our institution, but that doesn't mean I don't think it is the way to go
- freaking awesome...
- is greatly misunderstood!
- haven't tried it, but think it is a terrific option
- fun!
- not something supported by our consortium
- some support
- not permitted by my organization
- supported by a community with cool answer times (1–2 days)
- capable of evolving quickly
- not the same as free software
- not necessarily approved by management
- the obvious choice
- user driven, and flexible
- not totally free but less restrictive than proprietary.

Table A5 Types of open source software respondents use at home

What open source software do you use at home?	Total	%
None	66	6.76
Firefox	745	76.25
Thunderbird	183	18.73%
Gimp	282	28.86
VLC	201	20.57
FileZilla	139	14.23
Pidgin	115	11.77
OpenOffice	422	43.19
Adium	55	5.63
Zotero	196	20.06
Linux (Ubuntu or any other variation)	251	25.69
Other	151	15.46
Grand total	**2806**	

Figure A4 Types of open source software respondents use at home

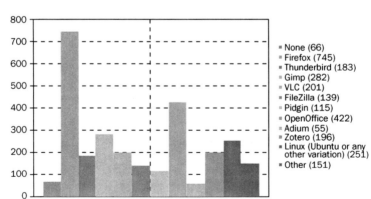

- None (66)
- Firefox (745)
- Thunderbird (183)
- Gimp (282)
- VLC (201)
- FileZilla (139)
- Pidgin (115)
- OpenOffice (422)
- Adium (55)
- Zotero (196)
- Linux (Ubuntu or any other variation) (251)
- Other (151)

Of the 66 people who answered that they don't use open source at home, 39 of them gave reasons:

- I was under the impression that OSS was only for computer whizzes, so stuck with (get ready for it) Microsoft!

- Don't manage computers at home.

- Needs are met with existing software.

- My husband is a PC tech and not as sold on open source as I am. He takes care of the home network, so he gets to choose what we use there.

- Don't have a need at this time but wouldn't hesitate if I did.

- I do not have a computer at home.

- Not enough time to research, set up, learn programs. But I do plan to look into an open source OPAC soon.

- The last thing I want to do at home is look at a computer!

- Never heard of any of these except Firefox & Linux. I don't do a lot of heavy computing at home since I stare at a screen all day at work.

- Do not have the need at home.

- Don't have time or interest.

- When I purchased my computer, it came with IE and the Microsoft Professional Office suite. I'm comfortable using those products and not motivated to change although intellectually I support open source products.

- Don't have Internet access.

- Not tech savvy.

- Not aware of its benefits.

- No time, little interest – when I come home from work using the computer is the last thing I want to do!

- What I'm using is adequate for my needs.

- I like IE.

- I'm not that savvy.

- I have no need. I would use Firefox, but many of the websites I use run better on IE.

- I don't have Internet access at home... can't afford it any more.

- I don't use Internet at home.

- The people I live with do not and it is easier not to load the open source software then deal with their frustrations.

- I've been re-directed to OpenOffice, but I didn't know anything about the reliability of open source applications. I will not incur any addition costs, and it was not clear who pays for OpenOffice. I don't enjoy sitting at and looking at the computer, and I certainly am not interested enough to learn a new office-type application!

- Don't know of any that would be of use to me.

- Don't feel that I am savvy enough and don't want to take the time to be so! Also, I just use my computer for basic stuff – email, bank account, bill pay, etc.

- Try not to compute at home.

- I do most of my work at work. I'm not a techie.

- Why would I?

- I get copies of work software for use on my work machine at home.

- Don't have a home computer. Get enough silliness at work.

- Don't care.

- I'm not a sophisticated computer user.

- In Nigeria, I am not financially ok to install one.

- Use home pc for email, light work.

- No computer.

- Never set any up.

- My husband runs our 'IT department' at home and he says I don't need it. He uses Firefox and Linux.

- Don't know enough about any of them. Don't know what I am missing.

Table A6 Why respondents use open source software at home rather than proprietary options

Why are you using the applications above at home over proprietary options?	Total	%
It's more cost effective	454	46.47
Works better than other options	523	53.53
Someone recommended it to me	208	21.29
It was the first thing I tried	38	3.89
I don't know	9	0.92
Other	143	14.64
Grand total	1,375	

Figure A5 Why respondents use open source software at home rather than proprietary options

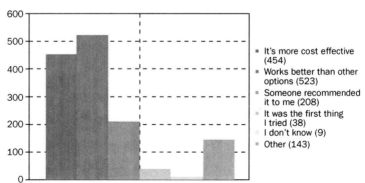

- It's more cost effective (454)
- Works better than other options (523)
- Someone recommended it to me (208)
- It was the first thing I tried (38)
- I don't know (9)
- Other (143)

Table A7	Types of open source software respondents use at work	

What open source software do you use at work?	Total	%
None	70	7.16
Firefox	715	73.18
Thunderbird	161	16.48
Gimp	210	21.49
VLC	96	9.83
FileZilla	150	15.35
Pidgin	106	10.85
OpenOffice	279	28.56
Adium	31	3.17
Zotero	161	16.48
Linux (Ubuntu or any other variation)	253	25.90
Koha	87	8.90
Evergreen	44	4.50
Kete	6	.61
SOPAC	7	.72
LibX	75	7.68
DSpace	100	10.24
WordPress	240	24.56
Drupal	187	19.14
Other	248	25.38
Grand total	3,226	

Figure A6	Types of open source software respondents use at work

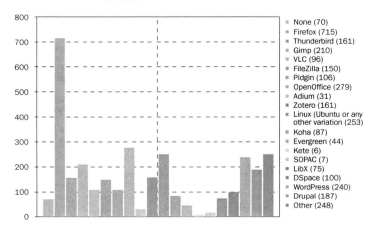

Of the 70 people who answered that they don't use open source at work, 49 of them gave reasons:

- No one asks for it.
- Too many network restrictions right now.
- I have decent tools with the software provided to me. Sure, there's stuff that could be better, but I don't have the authority to go off and change programs.
- My work is not willing to take any unnecessary steps other than fixing IE with weekly patches, on regular bases.
- The library does not currently have any OSS on their machines.
- Don't need to really.
- We haven't felt the need to switch to Firefox, and our computers came with installed software that has met our needs.
- See answer to previous question.
- The proprietary software offers what we need at this point.
- Not an option.
- IT won't allow us to install any OS software other than Firefox. However, our entire web site is migrating to Drupal in the next month.
- Can't download software without admin permissions, too difficult to incorporate into current ILS [integrated library system].
- They won't let us – I think they're afraid of it.
- IT people are REALLY particular as to what goes on with 'their' machines.
- Not allowed to use.

- Don't know of any that would be of use to me. Am trying with no success so far to install software to convert a map bar scale into a ratio.

- I prefer IE and we have a $000,000 ILS [integrated library system]!

- Unreliable, unproven and using a system which provides support.

- Some limitations due to network.

- We are looking into using open source for circulation.

- Not approved by corporate office.

- Recent graduate and not, yet, employed.

- Management is concerned that it is risky. There is a lack of understanding about what it is. There is reluctance to change or try new things.

- Boneheaded upper management and other institutional resistance.

- Too difficult to support. Lack of documentation. Lack of local knowledge.

- Not supported by our IT department.

- Too much trouble.

- Our library is controlled by the government.

- What we use is regulated by our IT department. Users don't make those decisions.

- For patron use, products like OpenOffice require extra steps to be compatible with MS Office, which is pervasive in schools and businesses (you have to know, or be told, to save documents in office formats in order to make them transferrable). ILS [integrated library system]: the systems just aren't there yet, and require expertise that is not necessarily available to all libraries.

- Not installed on computers there.

- Not my decision; not allowed.

- Haven't made the change for e-mail. For circulation and cataloging system, we are in a larger group of libraries that is using a costly provider.

- Because I can only use the software installed by my employer and they don't use open source.

- Because security is taken very serious (maybe too restrictive) and our former data processing center (Rechenzentrum) was outsourced and all the IT Service is now coming from an external service provider. The standard workplace is operated only with Windows and for every exception from the standard software you have to fill out an application and give an explanation... Just some months ago my Firefox browser was officially deleted from my desktop.

- Company policy.

- I've been exploring some – lack of DB provider tech support for problems getting into the programs, institutional regs about downloading unauthorized software.

- IT won't let us.

- Considered open source catalog; not supported. Other options available.

- We are investigating it, but no decision has been made yet.

- Would not be allowed by our IT, so I've never even considered it.

- I don't know enough about implementing software like Koha 2. Software and network administration is managed on an office-wide/corporate level.

- Haven't had a chance...

- My company dictates what I may use, and this far we have not adopted open source programs.

- IT department at work controls what we use.
- Our IT department has strict rules about downloading something without authorization.
- Not supported by my institution.
- Not sure if they would allow it, very PC here.
- Only programs allowed and approved by the company IT dept are used.

Table A8   Why respondents use open source software at work rather than proprietary options

Why are you using the applications above at work over proprietary options?	Total	%
It's more cost effective	463	47.39
Works better than other options	521	53.33
Someone recommended it to me	166	16.99
It was the first thing I tried	25	2.56
Work makes me use it	95	9.72
Other	150	15.35
Grand total	1,420	

Figure A7   Why respondents use open source software at work rather than proprietary options

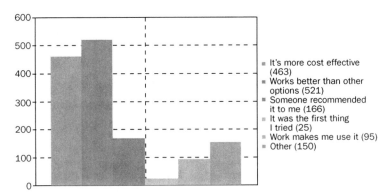

■ It's more cost effective (463)
■ Works better than other options (521)
■ Someone recommended it to me (166)
■ It was the first thing I tried (25)
■ Work makes me use it (95)
■ Other (150)

Final comments and quotes:

- Suggest ways for librarians to learn how to use open source & encourage the community to make it easier for first timer to learn, even without programming skills.

- We are currently seriously (attempting to put it up before August) looking into launching VuFind as our portal. We are also taking a serious look at Koha and Evergreen.

- I have an admitted bias against open source software because it varies so much in its reliability. Sometimes open source is free, sometimes it's the latest and greatest functionality, and sometimes people like to tweak it. I don't care about those things – most importantly, I have a library and/or a business to operate, and reliability is by far the paramount issue.

- I think it is especially important for archives to use non-proprietary software. It is a matter of long-term accessibility, to which we are supposed to be dedicated.

- Maybe given another decade, open source will have easier to install programs. Let's hope so.

- Given the choices listed as open source software, I gather that library IT staff is not your target audience for this survey.

- At work we don't have opportunities to choose and experiment with OS, unfortunately. Yes or no is decided by IT.

- I have been using open source applications for nearly 20 years. Some applications require a lot of local effort to customize and maintain, but most require no more effort than commercial software and many can be run right out of the box.

- At OSU Libraries, we are in the middle of a website infrastructure change, mostly moving towards open source software. Some of the big ones we use: SilverStripe CMS, Symfony, PHP5, Framework Doctrine ORM for PHP5, Lighttpd web server, Shibboleth SSO and WordPress MU. Since all of these are open source, I am able to modify the source to fully integrate them. Hope this helps the survey!

- Open source is a good idea but without someone or business working with it at a constant pace it's not able to keep up with the evil MS corporation. It also needs to be marketed to the public and once that starts it takes money and then all of a sudden you have another corporate software company. Until that changes I don't see how freeware will ever make it in the big time.

- Open source works best where there is a community of contributors who are committed to working with each other. This provides momentum and confidence for others considering adoption.

- Library schools with distance programs need to support free software!!!! I'm considering applying to library school and am tired of being told I need to purchase M$ Office with an academic discount.

- Survey is clearly biased to steer respondents toward answering in favor of open source software use, based on the options offered.

- Currently evaluating Koha (no production use) and will be taking a look at Kete. DSpace is excellent – we have just put it into production use. The Koha and DSpace communities need to be friends. My goal someday is to switch all our staff client computers from Windows to Linux.

- I believe that there is not sufficient support from library/institutions administrations and IT departments for the use of open source software.

- Managing risk is important, and using free/open source software gives organizations and individuals more control over their software and their data. Open standards are equally important, because they are one way of increasing the long-term viability of the data.

- It may be nice to look into some personal document management software (sort of like a personal library). I use Benubird PDF, which is only a free software not open source.

- We use a combination of proprietary and open source software. We are a smaller library with only one programmer and one web designer so are limited in what we can do. As time goes on and the open source becomes more fully developed we will likely use it more.

- Senayan Library Automation System (*http://senayan .diknas.go.id*) is very useful for me and my library, I use it with my Ubuntu server.

- Take care to research the history of the various free and open source software movements and distinguish between the various motivations for them. Free != open source != commons-licensed etc. I hope that's not painfully obvious, but many journalists and researchers conflate distinct sets of ethics that belong to very distinct populations. That's not helpful for anyone.

- Open source is a really exciting new direction for libraries, and one I feel is ripe for rapid take-up. UK does seem to be lagging behind, but I am hoping once we have a 'proof of concept' with VuFind, then we can explore the next logical step, which is a full OSS LMS system, possibly Koha, more likely Evergreen.

- Open source vs. closed source seems to be a false dichotomy. The pertinent questions are: is support available? Do we have developers on staff ready/able to extend the product if need be? How mature is the product? How active is the community? These 'total cost of ownership' considerations are the same between closed and open source. It's also important to take open data standards into account. This is a larger issue than source control.

- Our library seems willing to employ developers and use OSS for emerging applications (digital repositories, dig preservation), and in solid behind the scenes tasks (web servers, etc.), but when it comes to our ILS [integrated library system], I believe that only proprietary options are being considered. OSS does not fit existing tendering processes, and we don't seem to be adopting new processes that would accommodate evaluation of open source and proprietary solutions to determine which solution offers best value. The University is also trying to move towards a common computing environment that will be Windows-based – a very shortsighted move. We should focus more on interoperability and less on dictating what systems staff and students should use. I think the licensing aspect puts many institutions off developing and releasing OSS. There isn't much support available to help with this, although the OSS Watch group in the UK are now able to provide more guidance. JISC seem to be in favor of OSS, but I think they could do more to encourage UK HE and FE [higher education and further education] institutions to use it.

- I recently attended a conference with Amy de Groff as a keynote speaker (talking about Ubuntu at her library) and presentations on open source ILS used in Indiana. Academic libraries in the state (KY) are looking at open-source ILS as possible replacement for Voyager, which is the current system used by state-supported higher education institutions.

- I was lucky enough to take an open source software class at StudioXX in Montreal which is affordable and really believes in using OS over proprietary software. See *http://www.studioxx.org/en/courses*.

- I believe that open source is an important movement, especially in academic publishing. I take no pleasure in computer use, nor in web browsing: I use PC and web at home because there is no other good way to get some things done. Personal privacy is important to me; I am not likely to download any applications, and I NEVER make purchases over internet. Feel free to contact me as the 'reluctant user'.

- Open source and windows are both here to stay. Neither will supplant the other. Business will usually stick with MS for the ready support. Open source will continue to grow as zero initial cost to the public. Many feel Bill has too much market share (read that as control and money). I feel he has earned it and provided a great public service with MS products. Open source is fine, free of cost except sometime much time is required in certain situations.

- Open source is not for the weak of heart. However, people of all skill levels can use and contribute to open source software. It makes pioneers of all of us.

- I love the idea of open source ILS software, but am very skeptical about its ability to provide all that we have now in support and functionality for the same or less money. I'm hopeful that this will not always be the case.

- We are investigating Koha as a possible replacement for our very expensive and not very functional ILS, Symphony.

- I predict this survey will have no truly surprising results of the sort that might require reconsideration of one or more of the hypotheses being tested. And a survey constructed merely to confirm one's hypotheses (even if not explicitly intentionally so) falls into the category of 'Lies, damn lines, and statistics' in terms of its value to scholarly research.

- I hate Dspace but love Drupal and CUFTS. Not all open source is equal.

- We are on Classic Dynix and are searching for a new ILS for integration in 2010. We are at RFP finished and passed the board and now at the town lawyers and after that out for bid.

- Not sure how indicative this will be – it's a bit generic and doesn't question corporate/institutional attitude/acceptance of OS.

- Open source has much to offer libraries; the free exchange of information goes well with the free exchange of software.

- I'd use more open source software at work, but our IT department is fond of Microsoft.

- Also, use an open source VOIP software and video conferencing software. Looking in to using Kete, but may use Fedora instead for digital projects.

- We're very interested in open source as an idea, but are also aware that it is never 'free.' We want to look for the best supportable/sustainable performance we can provide for our users, no matter whether it is open source or proprietary. All other things being equal, we would prefer open source.

- The only reason I don't use more open source is that I was a corporate IT minion and they were using products that I had to support thus my time was better spent using the stuff they already picked.

- Open source = Good Commons.

- Am interested in open source ILMS systems in the future. We are the only open computer lab on campus (Information Commons) and are interested in any software that saves our students and the library's budget money.

- We are in the early stages of understanding and using Drupal for our back end content management of the website. Yet to launch it's still rather early to comment. I do like the customizing options with various modules. Think of an idea and there may be a module out there to use! Good community support both online and locally. Lots of libraries in our area are experimenting or will be using Drupal.

- The Open Disc Project is great! *http://www.theopendisc.com/*.

- I don't feel that I am very familiar with open source technology at all, but I don't really have much need for it at work or at home. (Unless I don't know what I'm missing?)

- I think this is a great idea. I hope you will not do a print book because the publication takes so long but will put out an easily accessible 'open' document on the results.

- I would love to use Koha and am trying to get to the point where we can, however there is no local support that knows Linux or Ubuntu and I myself do not know enough to run Ubuntu server. Cost is a huge factor for support, even if the software is free.

- My network is looking at an open source ILS for its next circulation system. I am excited.

- I love openoffice.org.

- Sonoma State University, in Cotati California used OSS on some of their library computers many years ago. This included Linux, web browsers, and simple utility software. For some reason, they have returned to the proprietary software world. Too bad...

■ I have made suggestions about using open source options in MPOW [my place of work]. The suggestions have been met with almost instant refusal due to the 'complications' of installing and customizing along with 'security issues.' Psh.

■ I volunteer in a ca 12,000-volume gay- and lesbian-oriented library. We present use Winnebago Spectrum as our online catalog. The program is no longer supported by the company that owns the software, Follett. Upgrading to Follett's current product, Destiny, would cost a minimum of $2,000, which we cannot afford. I desperately need to find software simply to do cataloging and circulation with; we have no acquisitions budget, so an ILS is unnecessary. It must run on the Windows platform. I've just discovered Koha, but have not had time to investigate.

■ I've been an advocate (though only briefly) for Linux in libraries. But my repeated finding is that software and hardware decisions are enmeshed with the parent institutions, which are slow or reluctant to change. Good luck, Nicole! I hope your book is able to persuade more libraries to go the open source route. It's certainly in keeping with our missions.

■ Open source is cost effective but requires intense customization. Many libraries may not have programmers or developers to develop the customized code required.

■ Any open source I use at work is fully unsupported by MPOW (my place of work). If there is a problem, IT department will not help and often asks me to uninstall it.

■ Have a look at PMB, it's very nice and flexible. See *http://www.sigb.net*.

- I am very interested in this topic. I am glad to see someone looking into it.

- There is much more training available for MS applications and other commercial applications. I want training in Joomla, and probably others that I don't even know about.

- I facilitate the New Services Committee. It was our committee's recommendation to install GIMP.ORG on one media PC at all locations, if the branch manager wanted it. We do have a concern about no control over what the customer edits on the program. It was recommended because it is cost effective. We also provide a tutorial CD for each PC where the software is installed.

- Open source is great although I was surprised how little I was actually using at home. I've only been into open source for about a year, so I still have a lot of stuff I use because, well, I'm familiar with it.

- We've looked at open source ILS systems, but do not have the expertise to adopt them yet (also must meet accessibility requirements of California).

- This is really cool idea. I've always been thinking about how libraries and open source go hand in hand.

- Our library is currently working on getting Drupal up and running as our CMS [content management system], but we've hit a few bumps in the road so it's taking longer than we'd hoped.

- In Indonesia, there are a software that use in library, named Senayan, you can see it in *http://senayan.diknas.ac.id/*.

- Open source definitely has its place in the library and in other areas as well. Too often, people who would otherwise support the implementation of an open source solution are turned off by over zealous supporters who make claims for open source that are questionable. Like most things in life, there needs to be a balance between things that can reasonably be supported in an open source model and those things which really do require a commercial/proprietary solution. In many cases, which model to choose will change over the course of time and that's the tricky part in making a decision between open source or not.

- Good luck on the project! I hope it helps lead to wider acceptance of open source software.

- I've been following the netbook market a little bit because my father travels a lot and I think this is a market that will flourish with open source OS. Also, I use the Google phone that is powered by Android, which is an OS that they are trying to configure for netbooks. I thought Google's video where they go into Times Square and ask people What is a Browser? was very telling... of course most people aren't using Firefox, chrome or browsers other than IE... do they even know there are other options? As more people learn about open source products, more people will use them. I introduce a lot of patrons to OpenOffice and Firefox.

- Open source is awesome. It would be great to discuss how to teach and advocate open source somewhere.

- Good luck! Please don't give up in this endeavor. Many libraries are looking for open source products to better utilize their OPACs. We do Not want to be forced into going with OCLC's WorldCat.local... Thanks!

- It should be noted I don't think open source is always the necessarily the 'best solution.' There are times that proprietary software does have the best solution. However, frequently it hits that sweet spot of cost, controllability, and enough of the needed feature set. The trade off is figuring out the problem is often difficult (but usually can be solved, where with closed source you just have to walk away), things can be in a rough state, and depending on distro updates seem to have a higher level of risk than some other closed source. The list of open source software I use though is huge. Just thought of another, imagemagick. I suppose if you really want a list I can dump my packages, although that will not tell you some of the stuff I've compiled from source...

- I would like to explore and use more open source applications at the library, but our director is not convinced there is enough support available. There is also a concern about the compatibility of MS Office 2007 with OpenOffice. As other libraries in Michigan move to Evergreen as a cost savings, I hope we also move in that direction as our current Sirsi/Dynix system is riddled with bugs and inconsistencies. As Evergreen has proven itself in GA and other states for many years as a stable and accurate system and I hope more libraries look toward open source software as a viable alternative to commercial system software.

- Take a look at our open source search engine 'Summa' at *http://www.statsbiblioteket.dk/summa*. The right column offers some information in English.

- I speak solely as myself and not on behalf of the library I work at.

- The most difficult thing in the case of Koha: maintaining (upgrading) and keeping up with new releases is challenging. The other thing is the cost of supporting Koha that companies demand is very high. It is beyond our budget. There is no support for Koha in Africa. The nearest is India.

- At work we usually work with MS Office, as most documents we receive are PDFs or MS Office documents. At work OpenOffice is not used so often. At home I only work with OpenOffice, this is ok as it does all I need. Internet Explorer unfortunately is used in our new library software; usually at work we use Firefox. OPUS is a software used for our publication server, MILESS does the same, it is used for special purposes.

- It's shocking to see that you didn't list NewGenLib in one of the open source products. I hope you know all the developments in this sector.

- I think, it'll be useful to make easier any Linux / open source software. Thus, easibility factor need to be improved.

- I am a big supporter of open source software. Currently the university is involved with the OLE (Open Library environment) project for creating an open source ILS. I took part in the initial workshops for creating the system, however my job duties have changed and I am not as involved.

- I hate dealing with licenses.

- I love hearing about others' experiences with open source ILSes, and really hope our library consortium considers open source options if/when we switch ILS.

- I've encouraged the use of open source software whenever possible. The cost of support is not overwhelming if you have a technically inclined person on hand. I find the use of Linux, Apache and PHP for a web server to be one of the easiest to maintain and set up.

- Most institutions are not supportive of moving off the Microsoft track even if staff is willing to go to open source, so we are stuck with MS products.

- Our library is looking into cheap, less powerful alternative to Photoshop®.

- I love the idea of open source. When it comes to library applications, we just don't have the manpower – we have a half position devoted to systems, the person in it is by necessity a librarian first, techie second, and he doesn't have the time to learn and support open source.

- I would love to be able to use more open source solutions here at the library (and suggest them often to admin), but have been realizing that open source isn't entirely free of cost – it requires staff time and money, which we are lacking.

- Our academic library is psyched to use open source software... the trouble is getting our IT folks on board.

- It's important to distinguish different kinds and qualities of open source projects. There is enormous variability.

- Events, like budget shortfalls, usually force libraries into innovative behavior. Like accountants, library managers believe that anything free is not worth the price. No one ever got fired for buying ContentDM or Encore. The open source desktops have become as good or better than Windows, but few libraries try to reap savings by using KDE or Gnome or XFCE. General open source software can easily be tweaked or customized, but few librarians or IT support people have the skill sets needed to do it well. Specialist open source software for libraries will require a support component that is not free. Open source will not be accepted in libraries until their masters in state and local government begin to use and believe in open source, but, much like responsible health care policy, we have yet to accept any European innovations in the workplace.

- I use a number of web and instructional applications that are open source, including but not limited to SlideRoll, Slideshow Maker, Poweroff 3.0, Google Chrome, etc.

- It would be good to ask if people are seriously considering using other open source products. We are looking at an ILS (Koha) but are still comparing systems and haven't implemented one yet.

- Kuali is a financial interface for universities and is much cheaper than buying a commercial product like Banner. Your questionnaire seemed targeted toward personal uses of open source software rather than institutional applications.

- I also love LimeSurvey.

- At work we are moving more and more to open source, are changing to an open source helpdesk software, planning to try an open source discovery layer and are exploring the possibility of an open source ILS in the future.

- We like Drupal. A lot. We also like Linux (CentOS), MySQL, Apache, PHP, Subversion and Margaritas (not software).

- Not sure why WordPress wasn't listed as a home option. Also, might have better analysis later if you asked more demographic questions – size [of] library, area of the country, etc. – and also asked if the library, not the person, used OSS (e.g. Apache, etc.).

- Only, that I am a firm believer in finding the right tool for the job. Sometimes that tool is open source, and sometimes it is better to use a commercial product.

- For me, FOSS shares a purpose with libraries – the sharing of information. The two have great potential together.

- I don't know what I'd do without portable open source software, since in-house restrictions prevent me from installing a lot of the software I need. I like to try out software first to see if it is really useful or not. If it is, I believe in contributing to the community, or donating monetarily, to help it continue.

- I'm a Machead, but I recently purchased a netbook that came (unfortunately) preloaded with Windows XP. I'm running Ubuntu from removable media simply for the challenge of learning something new. I hope to become sufficiently competent/confident with Ubuntu so that I can reformat the netbook as an Ubuntu-only machine. Why? Because I really like their philosophy: that Ubuntu and open source software make technology, access, and information accessible to all users regardless of financial or physical situations.

- I am new to open source and I think it is very exciting. Bill Gates has made enough money already.

- We use a lot of Google's offerings like Docs and the calendar.

- Libraries underestimate the cost in personnel required to support open source. Any cost savings on purchase or maintenance is just shifted to personnel. This may not be true for a small rural library who has an younger, eager techie available. But I wonder what happens when he gets a family and needs more competitive pay and perhaps moves away. In our situation as large library in a large metropolitan area, our IT salaries have to compete with the big corporations. We can't afford the knowledge we'd need to not have our ILS supported and developed by a whole vendor team.

- Librarians are rarely 'techy' enough to consider open source without some kind of support. Many of us are in our 50s and barely had computers in college, so we are not willing to transfer our whole automation process to something we don't understand.

- Open source software is a wonderful way to give patrons 'more'... more options, more services, etc. We installed Firefox on our public internet computers to give patrons a choice and OpenOffice in conjunction with Microsoft for the same reason. I use Firefox as my primary browser because of the customizations and flexibility and highly recommend it to anyone who listens! I would like to see more libraries adopt open source software, particularly those facing budget cuts.

- Also see our website at *http://meadvillelibrary.org/os* for info from presentations we have made at a number of conference, articles I've written, etc.

- Not enough information is out there about the 'costs' of open source. The software/code is free but there are definitely costs associated with use and maintenance.

- I think your survey is almost the equivalent of push polling.

- I would love to use open source in place of Microsoft Office but it would take more staff time to convince the patron who are used to the MS products. (Majority have limited experience and change is hard for them.) I have tried Firefox on public computers but found it is not ideal for that environment. But it's my own private browser of choice... so much better then IE.

- Before committing to Drupal I looked at several alternative CMS [content management system] options: Joomla, Plone, and Alfresco. If you want to know about Plone in libraries I'd suggest checking with the folks at the Plinkit Collaborative [at] *http://www.plinkit.org/* (some of them also presented at a past Code4Lib so check the conference archives).

- It's been fun watching the open source movement explode and become mainstream in libraries over the past few years. Many open source programs have such thriving user communities that make constant improvements and updates to the programs, making them the best of their kind – ie – Firefox! It appears that ILSs are headed in this direction as well, and that should be very interesting to watch over the next few years!

- This is just my personal experience, I'm sure it's not an exhaustive list of what's being used around here.

- We actually don't have a library in our school and there are no plans to build one. I teach technology and feel that part of my job is to be a resource for teaching research skills, validating information as well as a gateway of sorts to information on the internet.

- Sorry I don't even know what free source means. I am a grad student at Dominican and feel like I should know what that means, but...

- Support of the system is a problem for a small library without technology savvy staff.

- The biggest problem I have with open source stuff is how difficult it often is to get help figuring things out.

- DokuWiki has been quite handy as an mini-intranet for our staff, and Request Tracker has made dealing with staff requests much, much easier.

- I like the idea of open source. However, Joomla has been difficult to understand. I hope other open source software is not as difficult to utilize.

- I think open source is great, but I work for a library in a 75-member consortium that is not interested in exploring it at this time.

- We are fortunate to have an extremely skilled and savvy network manager who installed Ubuntu on our network and customized Koha for us. As a small public library director, I would not have been able to make time to learn how to do these things myself.

- We are currently converting to Koha, and I try to keep my knowledge up about open source by reading a number of blogs etc, so I am a dabbler, though a believer, in open source really. Koha is about to be our LMS for five of our seven libraries so we are learning fast.

- I believe to use open source is a trend in the library field. With little budget and more service needs, open source is a good solution for libraries.

- Our library is part of a small state agency that swings wildly between software types. We have elections every four years resulting in a new administration and a different way of doing things. First, the head of IT was a huge Microsoft person. Actually did some development on cutting edge stuff with Microsoft themselves. The next head of IT was HUGELY open source. One of the first proponents of open source in government. Then, the pendulum swung back and we are once again a Microsoft shop, but we do as we are told and do not innovate or ask for anything. One bowl of Microsoft gruel is good enough for us. Good Luck!

- The pay for support models created by proto-vendors arising from the increased use of FOSS will somehow morph into something all too familiar: the proprietary, company owned and developed, locked down, expensive to use...

- I'd like to use open source software but the court is very strict about security, as it should be.

Appendix 2 Web links

This appendix lists links from each chapter in alphabetical order. These links can be found on the official book website at *http://opensource.web2learning.net*.

Chapter 1

- Crowdsourcing (*http://crowdsourcing.typepad.com*)
- Firefox Web Browser (*http://firefox.com*)
- Free Software Foundation (*http://www.fsf.org*)
- GNU General Public License version 3 (GPLv3) (*http://www .opensource.org/licenses/gpl-3.0.html*)
- January 2010 Web Server Survey – Netcraft (*http://news.netcraft .com/archives/2010/01/07/january_2010_web_server_ survey.html*)
- Open Source Paradigm Shift (*http://www.oreillynet.com/ pub/a/oreilly/tim/articles/paradigmshift_0504.html*)
- OpenOffice.org (*http://www.openoffice.org*)
- The Free Software Definition (*http://www.gnu.org/philosophy/ free-sw.html*)

Chapter 2

- Assessing the Health of Open Source Communities (*http://floss.syr.edu/Presentations/oscon2006/2_Crowston*

2006Assessing%20the%20health%20of%20open%20 source%20communities.pdf)

- Crowdsourcing (*http://crowdsourcing.typepad.com*)

- Koha Open Source ILS (*http://koha-community.org*)

- Mentoring in Open Source Communities: What Works? What Doesn't? (*http://www.itworld.com/open-source/ 78271/mentoring-open-source-communities-what-works-what-doesnt*)

- Why Hackers Do What They Do: Understanding Motivation and Effort in Free/Open Source Software Projects (*http://opensource.mit.edu/papers/lakhaniwolf.pdf*)

Chapter 3

- From Free to Recovery (*http://www.opensource.org/node/471*)

- GSA Makes The Case For Open Source (*http://gcn.com/ blogs/tech-blog/2008/04/gsa-makes-the-case-for-open-source.aspx*)

- Internet Explorer Unsafe for 284 Days in 2006 (*http://blog .washingtonpost.com/securityfix/2007/01/internet_explorer_ unsafe_for_2.html*)

- January 2010 Web Server Survey – Netcraft (*http://news .netcraft.com/archives/2010/01/07/january_2010_web_ server_survey.html*)

- Top 5 Browsers from Jan 09 to Feb 10 (*http://gs.statcounter .com/#browser-ww-monthly-200901-201002-bar*)

Chapter 4

- Code of Ethics of the American Library Association (*http://www.ala.org/ala/aboutala/offices/oif/statementspols/ codeofethics/codeethics.cfm*)

- Drupal (*http://drupal.org*)
- Evergreen Open Source Library System (*http://open-ils.org*)
- Gift Cultures, Librarianship, and Open Source Software Development (*http://infomotions.com/musings/gift-cultures/*)
- Horowhenua Libraries (*http://www.library.org.nz*)
- Intranet 2.0: Fostering Collaboration with a Homegrown Intranet (*http://www.web2learning.net/publications-presentations/intranet-20-fostering-collaboration-with-a-homegrown-intranet*)
- Jenkins Law Library (*http://www.jenkinslaw.org*)
- Joomla (*http://www.joomla.org*)
- Koha Open Source ILS (*http://koha-community.org*)
- Open Source Software: Controlling Your Computing Environment (*http://infomotions.com/musings/oss4cil/index.shtml*)
- Open Source Solutions for Library Needs (*http://www.lugod.org/presentations/oss4lib.pdf*)
- The Importance of Open Access, Open Source, and Open Standards for Libraries (*http://istl.org/05-spring/article2.html*)

Chapter 5

- Jessamyn Installs Ubuntu (*http://vimeo.com/4169783*)
- Libstats (*http://code.google.com/p/libstats/*)
- LimeSurvey (*http://www.limesurvey.org*)
- Linux Online (*http://www.linux.org*)
- OpenOffice.org (*http://www.openoffice.org*)
- Ubuntu (*http://www.ubuntu.com*)

- VirtualBox (*http://www.virtualbox.org*)

- VirtualBox Forums (*http://forums.virtualbox.org*)

- What is Ubuntu? (*http://www.ubuntu.com/products/what isubuntu*)

- Why OpenOffice.org (*http://why.openoffice.org*)

Chapter 6

- Adblock Plus (*http://adblockplus.org*)

- Amazon.com (*http://www.amazon.com*)

- Barnes & Noble (*http://www.barnesandnoble.com*)

- Flashblock Add-on for Firefox (*https://addons.mozilla .org/en-US/firefox/addon/433*)

- Gmail IMAP Account Setup Add-on for Thunderbird (*https://addons.mozilla.org/en-US/thunderbird/addon/ 6381*)

- Google Scholar (*http://scholar.google.com*)

- Internet Explorer Unsafe for 284 Days in 2006 (*http:// blog.washingtonpost.com/securityfix/2007/01/internet_ explorer_unsafe_for_2.html*)

- LibX (*http://libx.org*)

- Lightning (*http://www.mozilla.org/projects/calendar/lightning/*)

- Nicole C. Engard on Zotero (*http://www.zotero.org/nengard*)

- NoScript Add-on for Firefox (*https://addons.mozilla.org/ en-US/firefox/addon/722*)

- Pidgin (*http://www.pidgin.im*)

- Plugins for Pidgin (*http://developer.pidgin.im/wiki/Third PartyPlugins*)

- Privacy & Security Add-ons for Firefox (*https://addons .mozilla.org/en-US/firefox/browse/type:1/cat:12*)

- Privacy and Security Add-ons for Thunderbird (*https:// addons.mozilla.org/en-US/thunderbird/browse/type:1/ cat:66*)

- Provider for Google Calendar Add-on for Thunderbird (*https://addons.mozilla.org/en-US/thunderbird/addon/ 4631*)

- Scriblio (*http://about.scriblio.net*)

- Security Fix (*http://voices.washingtonpost.com/securityfix/*)

- Thunderbird (*http://www.mozillamessaging.com/thunderbird*)

- Zotero (*http://www.zotero.org*)

- Zotero Compatible Standards & Software (*http://www .zotero.org/support/compatible_standards_and_software*)

- Zotero Research Guide (*http://research.library.gsu.edu/zotero*)

Chapter 7

- Audacity (*http://audacity.sourceforge.net*)

- Audio & Video Produced by the NYPL (*http://www.nypl .org/voices/audio-video*)

- CamStudio (*http://camstudio.org*)

- GIMP (*http://www.gimp.org*)

- GIMP Plugin Registry (*http://registry.gimp.org/list_content*)

- GIMPshop (*http://www.gimpshop.com*)

- Introduction to GIMP (*http://www.gimp.org/about/ introduction.html*)

- Koha Open Source ILS (*http://koha-community.org*)

- Lion & Serpent Journal Archive (*http://sekhetmaat.com/Journal/*)

- NExpress Tutorials (*http://www.nexpresslibrary.org/category/tutorial/*)

- RecordMyDesktop (*http://recordmydesktop.sourceforge.net/about.php*)

- Scribus Open Source Desktop Publishing (*http://www.scribus.net*)

Chapter 8

- Alexa the Web Information Company (*http://www.alexa.com*)

- Drupal (*http://drupal.org*)

- Drupal Case Studies (*http://drupal.org/cases*)

- Drupal Runs Three Times as Many Top Sites as the Next CMS (*http://tomgeller.com/content/drupal-runs-three-times-many-top-sites-next-cms*)

- Drupalib (*http://drupalib.interoperating.info*)

- FileZilla (*http://filezilla-project.org*)

- Howard County Library (*http://hclibrary.org*)

- Joomla (*http://www.joomla.org*)

- Joomla in Libraries (*http://www.joomlainlibrary.com*)

- Joomla! Community Showcase (*http://community.joomla.org/showcase/*)

- Library Success Wiki (*http://www.libsuccess.org/index.php?title=Open_Source_Software*)

- Linux.com (*http://www.linux.com*)

- MaiaCMS – Home (*http://maiacms.org*)

- MediaWiki (*http://www.mediawiki.org*)
- My Kansas Library on the Web (*http://www.mykansas library.org*)
- NEKLS (*http://www.nekls.org*)
- OpensourceCMS (*http://php.opensourcecms.com*)
- Practical Open Source Software for Libraries: Official Book Site (*http://opensource.web2learning.net*)
- The White House (*http://www.whitehouse.gov*)
- Whitehouse.gov using Drupal (*http://buytaert.net/white house-gov-using-drupal*)
- Wikipedia (*http://www.wikipedia.org*)
- WordPress (*http://wordpress.org*)
- WordPress for Libraries (*http://www.webjunction.org/706*)

Chapter 9

- DSpace (*http://dspace.org*)
- DSpace Add-ons (*http://dspace.org/add-ons-and-extensions/ addons/*)
- DSpace Use Case Examples (*http://dspace.org/use-case-examples/DSpace-Use-Cases.html*)
- Greenstone Digital Library Software (*http://www.greenstone .org*)
- Greenstone Digital Library Software Examples (*http://www .greenstone.org/examples*)
- Kete Horowhenua (*http://horowhenua.kete.net.nz*)
- Kete Horowhenua: The Story of the District as Told by its People (*http://kete.net.nz/blog/documents/show/33-kete-horowhenua-the-story-of-the-district-as-told-by-its-people*)

- Kete.net.nz (*http://kete.net.nz*)

- New Zealand Digital Library (*http://www.nzdl.org/cgi-bin/library.cgi*)

- ScholarSpace at University of Hawaii at Manoa (*http://scholarspace.manoa.hawaii.edu*)

- University of Waikato Library New Zealand Collections (*http://digital.liby.waikato.ac.nz*)

Chapter 10

- CUFTS (*http://researcher.sfu.ca/cufts*)

- CUFTS page for Technology & Operations Management (*http://cufts2.lib.sfu.ca/CRDB/BVAS/browse/facets/subject/594*)

- dbWIZ (*http://researcher.sfu.ca/dbwiz*)

- Following the Yellow Brick Road to Simplified Link Management (*http://www.web2learning.net/publications-presentations/following-the-yellow-brick-road-to-simplified-link-management*)

- GODOT (*http://researcher.sfu.ca/godot*)

- Ithaca College Library Research Guides: Computer Science (*http://www.ithacalibrary.com/sp/subjects/cs*)

- Libraries Stand Ready to Help in Tough Economic Times (*http://www.huffingtonpost.com/jim-rettig/libraries-stand-ready-to_b_150268.html*)

- Library à la Carte (*http://alacarte.library.oregonstate.edu*)

- Library à la Carte Forums (*http://alacarte.library.oregonstate.edu/forum*)

- Moodle (*http://moodle.org*)

- Open Knowledgebase (*http://researcher.sfu.ca/openkb*)

- reSearcher (*http://researcher.sfu.ca*)

- reSearcher at Chapman University (*http://cufts2.lib.sfu.ca/ CRDB/COU*)

- reSearcher Documents (*http://researcher.sfu.ca/documents*)

- SubjectsPlus (*http://www.subjectsplus.com*)

- SubjectsPlus at Middlebury (*http://www.middlebury.edu/ academics/lib/research/db-subject*)

- SubjectsPlus on Google Groups (*http://groups.google.com/ group/subjectsplus*)

- Whittier College Moodle (*http://cms.whittier.edu*)

Chapter 11

- Amazon.com (*http://www.amazon.com*)

- Athens County Public Libraries Catalog (*http://search .athenscounty.lib.oh.us*)

- Blacklight: Project Info (*http://rubyforge.org/projects/ blacklight/*)

- Collingswood Public Library (*http://collingswoodlib.org*)

- Darien Library Catalog (*http://www.darienlibrary.org/ catalog*)

- Designing an OPAC for Web 2.0 (*http://homepage.mac .com/misterbisson/Presentations/ALAMidwinter-2006Jan20.pdf*)

- Evergreen open source library system (*http://open-ils.org*)

- First-release! (*http://rubyforge.org/forum/forum.php?forum_ id=21035*)

- Georgia PINES Catalog (*http://gapines.org*)

- Georgia's 252 PINES Public Libraries Preparing Debut of Evergreen Software, Web-based Catalog (*http://www .librarytechnology.org/ltg-displaytext.pl?RC=12162*)

- Google Books (*http://books.google.com*)
- Horowhenua Libraries (*http://www.library.org.nz*)
- Kent County Public Library Catalog (*http://catalog .kentcountylibrary.org*)
- Koha Open Source ILS (*http://koha-community.org*)
- lib-web-cats (*http://www.librarytechnology.org/libwebcats/*)
- LibraryThing (*http://www.librarything.com*)
- Open Source Support for Libraries (*http://infomotions .com/tmp/oss/support.html*)
- Search Works (*http://searchworks.stanford.edu*)
- Search Works – Advanced Search (*http://searchworks.stanford .edu/advanced*)
- SOPAC 2 Released. Thesocialopac.net Launched. (*http://www .blyberg.net/2008/09/25/sopac-2-released-thesocial opacnet-launched/*)
- SOPAC2: The Social OPAC (*http://thesocialopac.net*)
- University of Virginia Library Catalog (*http://blacklight .betech.virginia.edu*)
- Villanova Falvey Memorial LIbrary Catalog (*https://library .villanova.edu/Find/*)
- Villanova University releases VUFIND, an open source next generation library catalog (*http://www.librarytechnology .org/ltg-displaytext.pl?RC=12664*)
- VuFind (*http://vufind.org*)
- W-E-B-S-I-T-E, Find Out What It Means To Me (*http://www .inthelibrarywiththeleadpipe.org/2009/w-e-b-s-i-t-e-find- out-what-it-means-to-me/*)

Appendix 3
Additional references

'4th Actuate Annual Open Source Survey Includes China; Attracts a Record Number of Responses,' June 22, 2009. *http://www.actuate.com/company/news/press-release/? articleid=17928*.

Abel, Rob. 'Will Open Source Software Become an Important Institutional Strategy in Higher Education?' Alliance for Higher Education Competitiveness, May 25, 2005. *http://www.a-hec.org/media/files/A-HEC_open_ source_0505.pdf*.

Acello, Richard. 'Opening Up to Open Source.' *ABA Journal* 94, no. 6 (June 2008): 32–34.

American Library Association. 'Code of Ethics of the American Library Association.' ALA, January 22, 2008. *http://www.ala.org/ala/aboutala/offices/oif/statementspols/ codeofethics/codeethics.cfm*.

'An Open Secret.' *Economist* 377, no. 8449 (October 22, 2005): 12–14.

Appleton, Karen, Dorothy DeGroot, Karen Lampe, and Cheryl Carruthers. 'Using "Moodle(TM)": how rural school librarians stay connected.' *School Library Monthly* 26, no. 2 (October 2009): 14–16.

Arne, Paul H., and John C. Yates. 'Open Source Software Licenses: perspectives of the end user and the software developer.' *Computer & Internet Lawyer* 22, no. 8 (2005): 1–13.

Balas, Janet L. 'Considering Open Source Software.' *Computers in Libraries* 24, no. 8 (2004): 36–39.

———. 'There's No Need to Fear Open Source.' *Computers in Libraries* 25, no. 5 (May 2005): 36–38.

Balnaves, E. 'Open Source Library Management Systems: a multidimensional evaluation.' *Australian Academic and Research Libraries* 39, no. 1 (2008): 1–13.

Bannerjee, Kyle. 'You Can Deliver the Goods Better, Faster, and Cheaper with Open Source Databases.' *Computers in Libraries* 25, no. 5 (2005): 16–22.

Barker, Stephen. 'Use your Moodle.' *Times Educational Supplement* 4791 (June 6, 2008): 30.

Beatty, Brian, and Connie Ulasewicz. 'Faculty Perspectives on Moving from Blackboard to the Moodle Learning Management System.' *TechTrends: linking research & practice to improve learning* 50, no. 4 (July 2006): 36–45.

Bissels, Gerhard. 'Implementation of an Open Source Library Management System: experiences with Koha 3.0 at the Royal London Homoeopathic Hospital.' *Program: Electronic Library & Information Systems* 42, no. 3 (July 2008): 303–314.

Bisson, Casey. 'Designing an OPAC for Web 2.0' presented at the ALA Midwinter, January 20, 2006. *http://homepage.mac.com/misterbisson/Presentations/ALAMidwinter-2006Jan20.pdf.*

Bisson, Casey, Jessamyn West, and Ryan Eby. 'Open-Source Software for Libraries.' *Library Technology Reports* 43, no. 3 (2007). *http://www.alatechsource.org/ltr/open-source-software-for-libraries.*

Blyberg, John. 'SOPAC 2 Released. Thesocialopac.net launched.' *blyberg.net*, September 25, 2008. *http://www.blyberg.net/2008/09/25/sopac-2-released-thesocialopacnet-launched/.*

Bonfield, Brett. 'W-E-B-S-I-T-E, Find Out What It Means To Me.' In the Library with the Lead Pipe, July 22, 2009. *http://www.inthelibrarywiththeleadpipe.org/2009/w-e-b-s-i-t-e-find-out-what-it-means-to-me/.*

Bove, Frank J. 'Creating Database-Backed Library Web Pages Using Open Source Tools.' *Portal: Libraries and the Academy* 7, no. 3 (July 2007): 385.

Boye, Janus, and Tony Byrne. 'Open Source Portals.' *EContent* 29, no. 6 (July 2006): 38–42.

Branzburg, Jeffrey. 'Use the Moodle Course Management System.' *Technology & Learning* 26, no. 1 (2005): 40.

Breeding, Marshall. 'An Update on Open Source ILS.' *Computers in Libraries* 27, no. 3 (March 2007): 27–29.

———. 'Making a Business Case for Open Source ILS.' *Computers in Libraries* 28, no. 3 (March 2008): 36–39.

———. 'Open Source and the ILS.' *Library Technology Reports* 40, no. 1 (January 2004): 84–85.

———. 'The Viability of Open Source ILS.' *Bulletin of the American Society for Information Science & Technology* 35, no. 2 (December 2008): 20–25.

Bretthauer, David. 'Open Source Software in Libraries.' *Library Hi Tech News* 18, no. 5 (June 2001): 8–9.

———. 'Open Source Software in Libraries: an update.' *Library Hi Tech News* 19, no. 5 (June 2002): 20–22.

Buytaert, Dries. 'Whitehouse.gov using Drupal.' *Dries Buytaert*, October 25, 2009. *http://buytaert.net/white house-gov-using-drupal.*

Caldwell, Tracey. 'Joy of the Open Road?' *Information World Review* 238 (2007): 18–20.

Cervone, Frank. 'The Open Source Option.' *Library Journal* 19 (2003): 8.

Cervone, H. Frank. 'Open Source Software to Support Distance Learning Library Services.' *Internet Reference Services Quarterly* 9, no. 3/4 (July 2004): 147–158.

Chavan, Abhijeet, and Shireen Pavri. 'Open-Source Learning Management with Moodle.' *Linux Journal* 128 (December 2004): 66–70.

Chawner, Brenda. 'Koha: an open source success story.' *Library Link*, November (2002). *http://mustafa.emerald insight.com/vl=12220074/cl=48/nw=1/rpsv/librarylink/technology/nov02.htm.*

Chawner, Brenda, and Nicole C. Engard. 'Free/Libre and Open Source Software and Libraries Bibliography,' 2010. *http://www.zotero.org/groups/freelibre_and_open_source_software_and_libraries_bibliography.*

Chudnov, Daniel. 'Libraries in Computers: what librarians still don't know about open source.' *Computers in Libraries* 28, no. 3 (2008): 40.

———. 'Open Source Software: the future of library systems?' *Library Journal* 124, no. 13 (August 1, 1999): 40.

Clark, John. 'The Internet Connection: open source library software – ready for prime time?' *Behavioral & Social Sciences Librarian* 27, no. 3/4 (December 2008): 211–213.

Clarke, Kevin S. 'Open Software and the Library Community.' University of North Carolina – Chapel Hill, School of Information and Library Science, 2000.

Coffe, Peter. 'Open-source Model Opens Up Options.' *eWeek* 22, no. 7 (February 14, 2005): D4.

Colford, Scot. 'Explaining Free and Open Source Software.' *Bulletin of the American Society for Information Science & Technology* 35, no. 2 (December 2008): 10–14.

Corrado, Edward M. 'The Importance of Open Access, Open Source, and Open Standards for Libraries.' *Issues in Science and Technology Librarianship* 42 (Spring 2005). *http://istl.org/05-spring/article2.html.*

Corrado, Edward M., and Kathryn A. Frederick. 'Free and Open Source Options for Creating Database-Driven Subject Guides.' *The Code4Lib Journal*, April 10, 2008. *http://journal.code4lib.org/articles/47.*

Crawford, Richard. 'Open Source Solutions for Library Needs' presented at the Linux Users Group of Davis, December 5, 2003. *http://www.lugod.org/presentations/oss4lib.pdf.*

Critz, Lori, and Larry Hansard. 'Discovery Tool VUFind: Georgia Tech's implementation enhances findability of resources' presented at the GUGM (GIL Users Group Meeting), Fort Valley, Georgia, May 15, 2008. *http://smartech.gatech.edu/handle/1853/21586.*

Crowston, Kevin, and James Howison. 'Assessing the Health of Open Source Communities.' *IEEE Computer* 39, no. 5 (2006): 89–91.

Darby, Andrew. 'Implementing an Open Source Application in a College Library: ECU's pirate source.' *College & Undergraduate Libraries* 13, no. 1 (June 2006): 41.

'Development Stats for the Entire History of the Koha Project.' *http://stats.workbuffer.org/koha-combined-history/index.html.*

DiBona, Chris, Sam Ockman, and Mark Stone, eds. *Open Sources: voices from the open source revolution.* Sebastopol, CA: O'Reilly Media, Inc., 1999.

'DSpace Use Case Examples.' *DSpace. http://dspace.org/use-case-examples/DSpace-Use-Cases.html.*

Duffett-Smith, James. 'How to Use Open Source with Confidence.' *Computer Weekly* (April 25, 2006): 22.

Economides, Nicholas, and Evangelos Katsamakas. 'Two-Sided Competition of Proprietary vs. Open Source Technology Platforms and the Implications for the Software Industry.' *Management Science* 52, no. 7 (July 2006): 1057–1071.

Ellaway, Rachel, and Ross D. Martin. 'What's Mine Is Yours: open source as a new paradigm for sustainable healthcare education.' *Medical Teacher* 30, no. 2 (March 2008): 175–179.

Engard, Nicole C, and RayAna M Park. 'Intranet 2.0: fostering collaboration.' *Online* 30, no. 3 (2006): 16.

Eyler, Pat. 'Koha: a gift to libraries from New Zealand.' *Linux Journal* 106 (2003): 1.

Fontana, Richard. 'The Free Software Way.' *Groklaw*, January 26, 2010. *http://www.groklaw.net/article.php?story=20100126135326412.*

Fox, Robert. 'Digital Libraries: the system analysis perspective.' *OCLC Systems & Services* 22, no. 2 (May 2006): 100–106.

Free Software Foundation, Inc. 'GNU General Public License version 3 (GPLv3).' *Open Source Initiative*, June 29, 2007. *http://www.opensource.org/licenses/gpl-3.0.html.*

Garsten, Christina, and Helena Wulff. *New Technologies at Work: people, screens, and social virtuality.* Oxford and New York: Berg, 2003.

Geller, Tom. 'Drupal Runs Three Times as Many Top Sites as the Next CMS.' *Tom Geller's Latest Thing*, January 18, 2010. *http://tomgeller.com/content/drupal-runs-three-times-many-top-sites-next-cms.*

'Georgia's 252 PINES Public Libraries Preparing Debut of Evergreen Software, Web-based Catalog.' Library Technology Guides, August 21, 2006. *http://www.librarytechnology.org/ltg-displaytext.pl?RC=12162.*

Goldsborough, Reid. 'Is it Time to Switch to Open-Source Software?' *Black Issues in Higher Education* 22, no. 10 (June 30, 2005): 33.

González-Barahona, Jesús M., Joaquín Seoane Pascual, and Gregorio Robles. *Introduction to Free Software.* 3rd ed. Fundacio? per a la Universitat Oberta de Catalunya, 2009. *http://ftacademy.org/materials/fsm/1#1.*

Goode, Sigi. 'Something for Nothing: management rejection of open source software in Australia's top firms.' *Information & Management* 42, no. 5 (July 2005): 669–681.

Gooding, Sarah. 'WordPress as a Learning Management System: Move Over, Blackboard.' *WPMU.org*, February 1, 2010. *http://wpmu.org/wordpress-as-a-learning-management-system-move-over-blackboard/*.

Gordon, Rachel Singer, and Jessamyn West. 'What Can Open Source Do for You?' *Computers in Libraries* 28, no. 3 (March 2008): 44–45.

Gourley, Don. 'Open Source Software, Increasingly Used in Libraries, Could be an Inexpensive Solution to Making the Pieces of Your System Fit Together Better. Is it right?' *Computers in Libraries* 20, no. 9 (2000): 40.

Griggs, Kim. 'Library Information Made to Order: an open source project built for and with librarians.' *Computers in Libraries* 29, no. 2 (February 2009): 12–47.

Griggs, Kim, and Jane Nichols. 'Library à la Carte: customize|collaborate|connect overview & demo.' Presentation at the OCLC Research Technical Advances for Innovation in Cultural Heritage Institutions Webinar Series, August 2009. *http://ir.library.oregonstate.edu/jspui/handle/1957/12728*.

Guess, Andy. 'Outsourcing, Open Source and Budget Cuts.' *Inside Higher Ed*, October 29, 2008. *http://www.insidehighered.com/news/2008/10/29/computing*.

Guhlin, Miguel. 'Open Source and ROI.' *Technology & Learning* 27, no. 12 (July 2007): 12–14.

———. 'The Case for Open Source.' *Technology & Learning* 27, no. 7 (February 2007): 16–21.

Harper, Eliot. 'Scribus: open source desktop publishing.' *Seybold Report: Analyzing Publishing Technologies* 9, no. 1 (January 8, 2009): 7–14.

Hars, Alexander, and Shaosong Qu. 'Working for Free? motivations for participating in open-source projects.' *International Journal of Electronic Commerce* 6, no. 3 (Spring 2002): 25.

Hassett, Robert E. 'The Chapel Hill Linux Lab: a case study in the use of Linux and other open source applications in the high school setting.' University of North Carolina – Chapel Hill, School of Information and Library Science, 2002.

Herrington, Vee. 'Open Source Information and the Military Intelligence Library.' *Military Intelligence Professional Bulletin* 31, no. 4 (October 2005): 30.

Horner, Perry C. 'Linux for Public Workstations.' In *LITA National Forum*. St. Louis, MO, 2004. *http://www.ala.org/ala/lita/litaevents/2004Forum/CS_Linux_Client_Creation.pdf*, *http://www.ala.org/ala/lita/litaevents/2004Forum/CS_Linux_West_Library.pdf* and *http://www.ala.org/ala/lita/litaevents/2004Forum/CS_Linux_Final.pdf*.

Horton, Glen. 'Open Source Software for Libraries' presented at the Computers in Libraries conference, Washington, DC, 2006. *http://www.infotoday.com/cil2006/presentations/B303_Horton.html*.

Houser, John. 'Open Source Operating Systems in Libraries.' *Library Technology Reports* 45, no. 3 (April 2009): 8.

———. *Open Source Public Workstations in Libraries*. Vol. 45. Library Technology Reports. Chicago: ALA, 2009. *http://www.alastore.ala.org/detail.aspx?ID=2830*.

———. 'The VuFind Implementation at Villanova University.' *Library Hi Tech* 27, no. 1 (2009): 93–105.

———. 'Why Look at Open Source Now?' *Library Leadership Network*, July 28, 2009. *http://lln.lyrasis.org/node/374*.

Howe, Jeff. *Crowdsourcing: why the power of the crowd is driving the future of business*. New York: Crown Business, 2008. *http://crowdsourcing.typepad.com/*.

Huwe, Terence. 'Building Digital Libraries: open source, meet user-generated science.' *Computers in Libraries* 29, no. 2 (2009): 19.

'Introduction to GIMP.' *GIMP*, 2009. *http://www.gimp.org/about/introduction.html*.

Jackson, Joab. 'GSA Makes the Case for Open Source.' *Government Computer News*, April 16, 2008. *http://gcn .com/blogs/tech-blog/2008/04/gsa-makes-the-case-for-open-source.aspx.*

'January 2010 Web Server Survey.' *Netcraft*, January 7, 2010. *http://news.netcraft.com/archives/2010/01/07/january_2010_web_server_survey.html.*

Jaschik, Scott. 'The Next Open Source Movement.' *Inside Higher Ed*, July 6, 2009. *http://www.insidehighered.com/news/2009/07/06/kuali.*

Jones, Richard, and Theo Andrew. 'Open Access, Open Source and E-theses: the development of the Edinburgh Research Archive.' *Program: Electronic Library & Information Systems* 39, no. 3 (July 2005): 198–212.

Jordan, Elizabeth. 'LibStats.' *Performance Measurement and Metrics* 9, no. 1 (2008): 18.

Kachmar, Diane. 'Open Source Software and Libraries: is a revolution brewing?' *Information Technology & Libraries* 18, no. 4 (December 1999): Iv.

Kapor, Mitchell. 'How Is Open Source Special?' *Educause Review* 40, no. 2 (March 2005): 72–73.

Kauffman, Nicole. 'Moodle Offers Model for High-tech Classroom Learning, Discussions.' *Herald-Times*, December 18, 2006.

Kidman, Angus. 'NZ School Ditches Microsoft and Goes Totally Open Source: education, Linux, linux.conf.au, Microsoft – CIO,' January 25, 2010. *http://www.cio .com.au/article/333686/nz_school_ditches_microsoft_goes_totally_open_source?pp=1.*

King, David, Jessica Kopecky Tipton, and Heather Hill. 'KCResearch: creating a research portal using open source technology.' *Public Library Quarterly* 24, no. 3 (July 2005): 63–73.

Koontz, Brian. 'Open Source Technology: meeting the needs of the future of IT.' *Community College Week* 18, no. 16 (March 13, 2006): 6.

Krebs, Brian. 'Internet Explorer Unsafe for 284 Days in 2006.' *The Washington Post: Security Fix*, January 4, 2007. *http://blog.washingtonpost.com/securityfix/2007/01/internet_explorer_unsafe_for_2.html*.

Krichel, T. 'From Open Source to Open Libraries.' *Bulletin: American Society for Information Science and Technology* 35, no. 2 (2009): 39–46.

Krill, Paul. 'Warming to Open Source.' *InfoWorld* 26, no. 47 (November 22, 2004): 18.

Krishnamurthy, M. 'Open Access, Open Source and Digital Libraries: a current trend in university libraries around the world.' *Program: Electronic Library & Information Systems* 42, no. 1 (February 2008): 48–55.

Lakhani, Karim R, and Bob Wolf. 'Why Hackers Do What They Do: understanding motivation and effort in free/open source software projects.' Free/Open Source Research Community, September 2009. *http://opensource.mit.edu/papers/lakhaniwolf.pdf*.

Laoubani, Tarek, Alison Sinclair, Sally Murray, Claire Kendall, Anita Palepu, Anne Marie Todkill, and John Willinsky. 'No Budget, No Worries: free and open source publishing software in biomedical publishing.' *Open Medicine* 2, no. 4 (2008). *http://www.openmedicine.ca/article/viewArticle/276/211*.

Lerner, J., and J. Tirole. 'Some Simple Economics of Open Source.' *Journal of Industrial Economics* 50, no. 2 (2002): 197–234.

Lewis, Paul H. 'Why Linux works for Libraries.' *Computers in Libraries* 22, no. 10 (2002): 28–30, 32–35.

Library and Information Technology Association. *Open Source Software for Libraries: an open source for libraries collaboration*. Chicago: LITA, 2002.

Library and Information Technology Association. *Major Open Source Web Finding Tools and Digital Library Systems for Librarians*. Palm Desert, CA: American Library Association, 2002.

Library of Congress. 'Library Explores Ways to Release Open Source Software.' Library Technology Guides, January 14, 2010. *http://www.librarytechnology.org/ltg-displaytext.pl?RC=14498*.

Lucia, Joe. 'Song of the Open Road' presented at the Evergreen International Conference, Athens, GA, May 2009. *http://www.slideshare.net/evergreenils/joe-lucia-song-of-the-open-road*.

———. 'Villanova University Releases VUFIND, an Open Source Next Generation Library Catalog.' Library Technology Guides, July 15, 2007. *http://www.library technology.org/ltg-displaytext.pl?RC=12664*.

Madden, Maryna Jean. 'Today's UK Professional Association Library and Information Service.' *Aslib Proceedings* 60, no. 6 (2009): 556.

Mah, Calvin. 'dbWiz: open source federated searching for academic libraries.' *Library Hi Tech* 23, no. 4 (December 1, 2005): 490–503.

Marmion, Dan. 'The Open Source Movement and Libraries.' *Information Technology and Libraries* 20, no. 4 (2001): 171.

Maurer, Stephen, and Suzanne Scotchmer. 'Open Source Software: the new intellectual property paradigm,' March 22, 2006. *http://socrates.berkeley.edu/~scotch/maurer_and_scotchmer_oss.pdf*.

McDonald, Robert H., and Catherine M. Jannik. 'From Web Server to Portal: one library's experience with open source software.' *Journal of Library Administration* 40, no. 1/2 (February 2004): 71–88.

Mellinger, Margaret. 'Research Guides Remixed.' Presentation at the American Library Association Annual, Anaheim, CA, July 2008. *http://scholarsarchive .library.oregonstate.edu/jspui/handle/1957/8950*.

Mellinger, Margaret, Jane Nichols, and Kim Griggs. 'To Build or Buy: the tale of the Library à la Carte™ Open Source Project.' Presentation at the American Library Association Annual, Chicago, IL, July 2009. *http://ir.library .oregonstate.edu/jspui/handle/1957/12090*.

Menzies, Kathleen, and University of Strathclyde, Scottish Library and Information Council. *Open Source Library Management Systems Open Source Software, Smart Cards and Public Libraries in Scotland: a survey of the landscape, in context: a report undertaken by Kathleen Menzies.* Glasgow: Centre for Digital Library Research, 2009.

Mickey, Bill. 'An Interview with Dan Chudnov.' *Online 25*, no. 1 (January 2001): 23.

Miller, Ron. 'Open source CMS Edges Toward the Mainstream.' *EContent* 28, no. 1/2 (January 2005): 32–36.

Mitatek, Hunter. 'Open Source? You're Soaking in IT.' *Network Computing* 17, no. 5 (March 16, 2006): 12.

Mitchell, Erik, and Kevin Gilbertson. 'Using Open Source Social Software as Digital Library Interface.' *D-Lib Magazine* 14, no. 3/4 (3, 2008). *http://www.dlib.org/dlib/ march08/mitchell/03mitchell.html*.

Mockus, Audris, Roy Fielding, and James Herbsleb. 'Two Case Studies of Open Source Software Development: Apache and Mozilla.' *ACM Transactions on Software Engineering and Methodology* 11, no. 3 (July 2002): 309–346.

Moe, Tammi. 'Open Source Software and Thin-Client Networking – economical alternatives for public libraries.' *Public Libraries* 43, no. 5 (2004): 291.

Mohamed, Arif. 'Users Need to Work More Closely with the Open Source Community, says Forrester.' *Computer Weekly* (October 18, 2005): 26.

Molyneux, Robert. 'Evergreen in Context.' *Bulletin of the American Society for Information Science & Technology* 35, no. 2 (December 2008): 26–30.

Morgan, Eric Lease. 'Gift Cultures, Librarianship, and Open Source Software Development,' November 14, 2004. *http://infomotions.com/musings/gift-cultures/.*

———. 'Introduction: open source software in libraries.' *Bulletin of the American Society for Information Science & Technology* 35, no. 2 (December 2008): 8–9.

———. 'Open Source Software: controlling your computing environment,' March 28, 2009. *http://infomotions.com/musings/oss4cil/index.shtml.*

———. 'Possibilities for Open Source Software in Libraries.' *Information Technology & Libraries* 21, no. 1 (March 2002): 12.

Moses, Donald, and Jennifer Richard. 'Solutions for Subject Guides.' *Partnership: The Canadian Journal of Library and Information Practice and Research* 3, no. 2 (December 21, 2008). *http://journal.lib.uoguelph.ca/index.php/perj/article/viewArticle/907/1351.*

'NewGenLib: an open source ILS for Libraries in the developing world.' *Smart Libraries* 28, no. 3 (2008): 3.

'News in Brief: PINES Consortium.' *Advanced Technology Libraries* 33, no. 9 (2004): 11.

Nichols, Jane. 'Library à la Carte.' *College & Research Libraries News* 70, no. 5 (May 2009): 280.

O'Reilly, Tim. 'Lessons from Open-source Software Development.' *Communications of the ACM* 42, no. 4 (April 1999): 32–37.

———. 'Open Source Paradigm Shift.' *O'Reilly Media*, June 2004. *http://www.oreillynet.com/pub/a/oreilly/tim/articles/paradigmshift_0504.html*.

O'Reilly, Tim, and Library and Information Technology Association. *Practical Solutions for Libraries' Open Source Software*. Chicago, IL: American Library Association.

'Open Source ILS Gains Ground with Academic Libraries.' *Smart Libraries* 28, no. 2 (2008): 1.

'Open Source in an Academic University Library.' *Online* 25, no. 1 (January 2001): 21.

'Open Source Open World.' *Focus*, February 2010. *http://www.focus.com/fyi/information-technology/open-source-open-world/*.

'Open Source Popular at U.K. Universities.' *Educause Review* 41, no. 5 (September 2006): 6–8.

Owen, G. W. Brian, and Kevin Stranack. 'The Public Knowledge Project and the Simon Fraser University Library: a partnership in open source and open access.' *Serials Librarian* 55, no. 1/2 (2008): 140–167.

Pace, Andrew K. 'Free and Freedom.' *American Libraries* 38, no. 8 (September 2007): 44.

Parry, Marc. 'After Losing Users in Catalogs, Libraries Find Better Search Software.' *The Education Digest* 75, no. 6 (February 2010): 54.

Pavlicek, Russell. *Embracing Insanity: open source software development*. Indianapolis, IN: SAMS, 2000.

Perens, B. 'The Open Source Definition.' *Open Sources: voices from the open source revolution* (1999): 171–188.

Poynder, Richard. 'The Open Source Movement.' *Information Today* 18, no. 9 (October 2001): 1.

Proffitt, Brian. 'Koha: a library checks out open source,' September 4, 2002. *http://www.linuxplanet.com/linux planet/reports/4408/1/*.

Puckett, Jason. 'Superpower Your Browser with LibX and Zotero.' *College & Research Libraries News* 71, no. 2 (February 2010): 70–97.

———. 'Zotero Research Guide.' Library Research Guides at Georgia State University. *http://research.library.gsu.edu/zotero*.

Rafiq, M. 'Issues and Lessons Learned in Open Source Software Adoption in Pakistani Libraries.' *Electronic Library* 27, no. 4 (2009): 601–610.

Rafiq, Muhammad. 'LIS Community's Perceptions Towards Open Source Software Adoption in Libraries.' *International Information & Library Review* 41, no. 3 (2009): 137.

Ransom, Joann. 'Kete Horowhenua' presented at the BridgingWorlds Conference held in Singapore on October 17, 2008. Kete.net.nz, October 2008. *http://kete.net.nz/site/documents/show/42-kete-horowhenua-presented-at-the-bridgingworlds-conference-held-in-singapore-on-the-17th-october-2008*.

———. 'Kete Horowhenua: the story of the district as told by its people.' Kete.net.nz, February 2008. *http://kete.net.nz/blog/documents/show/33-kete-horowhenua-the-story-of-the-district-as-told-by-its-people*.

———. 'The Cost Effectiveness of Open Source for HLT.' *Library Matters*, December 4, 2009. *http://library-matters.blogspot.com/2009/12/cost-effectiveness-of-open-source-for.html*.

Rapoza, Jim. 'Open-source Support.' *eWeek* 21, no. 16 (April 19, 2004): 52.

Raymond, Eric S. *The Cathedral and the Bazaar: musings on Linux and open source by an accidental revolutionary.* O'Reilly & Associates, Inc., 2001.

Rettig, Jim. 'Libraries Stand Ready to Help in Tough Economic Times.' *The Huffington Post*, December 11,

2008. *http://www.huffingtonpost.com/jim-rettig/libraries-stand-ready-to_b_150268.html.*

Rhyno, Art. *Using Open Source Systems for Digital Libraries.* Westport, CO, and London: Libraries Unlimited, 2003.

Riley, John. 'Open Source Given the Thumbs Up as Viable Alternative by Whitehall.' *Computer Weekly* (June 28, 2005): 10.

Rosen, Franca. 'Evergreen: built for a consortium.' *Library Journal* 130 (Spring 2005): 7.

Rosenberg, Donald K. *Open Source: the unauthorized white papers.* Hungry Minds, 2000.

Sadler, Bess. 'First Release!.' *RubyForge: Blacklight*, January 26, 2008. *http://rubyforge.org/forum/forum.php?forum_id=21035.*

Sadler, Elizabeth (Bess). 'Project Blacklight: a next generation library catalog at a first generation university.' *Library Hi Tech* 27, no. 1 (2009): 57–67.

Schindler, Esther. 'Mentoring in Open Source Communities: what works? what doesn't?' *Itworld* (September 20, 2009). *http://www.itworld.com/open-source/78271/mentoring-open-source-communities-what-works-what-doesnt.*

Schneider, K. G. 'The Thick of the Fray: open source software in libraries in the first decade of this century.' *Bulletin of the American Society for Information Science & Technology* 35, no. 2 (December 2008): 15–19.

Schrock, Thor. 'Open-Source Programs vs. Fee-Based Applications: how do they stack up?' *Smart Computing* 18, no. 3 (March 2007): 33–36.

Sheehan, Kate. 'Creating Open Source Conversation.' *Computers in Libraries* 29, no. 2 (February 2009): 8–11.

Shirky, Clay. *Here Comes Everybody: the power of organizing without organizations.* New York: Penguin Press, 2008.

Sisler, Eric. 'Linux in your Library?' *Library Journal* (Fall 2001): 12–14.

Sonker, Sharad Kumar, and Francis Jayakanth. 'Koha: an open source integrated library automation system.' *SRELS Journal of Information Management* 40, no. 2 (2003): 135–146.

Stencel, Mark. 'The Open-Minded Desktop.' *Governing* 20, no. 4 (January 2007): 52.

Stephens, Michael. 'All About Podcasting.' *Library Media Connection* 25, no. 5 (February 2007): 54–57.

Stewart, Brian, Derek Briton, Mike Gismondi, Bob Heller, Dietmar Kennepohl, Rory McGreal, and Christine Nelson. 'Choosing Moodle: an evaluation of learning management systems at Athabasca University.' *International Journal of Distance Education Technologies* 5, no. 3 (July 2007): 1–7.

Stranack, Kevin. 'CUFTS: an open source alternative for serials management.' *Serials Librarian* 51, no. 2 (2006): 29–40.

———. 'The reSearcher Software Suite: a case study of library collaboration and open source software development.' *Serials Librarian* 55, no. 1/2 (2008): 117–139.

'Surveying the Open-source Landscape in Higher Ed.' *Educause Review* 41, no. 3 (May 2006): 6.

Tennant, Roy. 'Open Source Goes Mainstream.' *Library Journal* 128, no. 13 (2003): 30.

———. 'The Role of Open Source Software.' *Library Journal* 125, no. 1 (2000): 36.

———. 'VuFind Rocks the House.' blog, *Digital Libraries* (July 19, 2007). *http://www.libraryjournal.com/blog/1090000309/post/1050012105.html*.

Terlaga, Amy. 'Fear and Trembling in Connecticut: (or "how I learned to stop worrying and love open source").' *Computers in Libraries* 30, no. 1 (2010): 13.

Tiemann, Michael. 'From Free to Recovery.' *Open Source Initiative*, September 28, 2009. *http://www.opensource.org/node/471*.

'Top 5 Browsers from Jan 09 to Feb 10.' *StatCounter Global Stats*, February 19, 2010. *http://gs.statcounter.com/ #browser-ww-monthly-200901-201002-bar.*

Trainor, Cindi. 'Open Source, Crowd Source: harnessing the power of the people behind our libraries.' *Program: Electronic Library & Information Systems* 43, no. 3 (2009): 288–298.

Van Rooij, Shahron Williams. 'Perceptions of Open Source Versus Commercial Software: is higher education still on the fence?' *Journal of Research on Technology in Education* 39, no. 4 (2007): 433–453.

Wallis, Kim. 'The Next Generation Online Public Access Catalog in Academic Libraries.' *Open and Libraries Class Journal* 1, no. 2 (November 2, 2009). *http://www.infosherpas .com/ojs/index.php/openandlibraries/article/view/29/36.*

Wayner, Peter. *Free For All: how Linux and the free software movement undercut the high-tech titans.* New York: Harper Business, 2000.

Weber, Steve. *The Success of Open Source.* Cambridge, MA: Harvard University Press, 2004.

'What is Ubuntu?' *Ubuntu*, 2010. *http://www.ubuntu.com/ products/whatisubuntu.*

Whitehurst, Jim. 'Open Source: narrowing the divide between education, business, and community.' *EDUCAUSE Review* 44, no. 1 (February 2009): 70–71.

'Why OpenOffice.org.' *OpenOffice.org*, 2009. *http://why .openoffice.org/.*

Witten, Ian H., Matt Jones, David Bainbridge, Polly Cantlon, and Sally Jo Cunningham. 'Digital Libraries for Creative Communities.' *Digital Creativity* 15, no. 2 (June 2004): 110–125.

Yang, Sharon, Meghan Weeks, and Melissa A. Hofmann. 'Koha, Evergreen, and Voyager: a comparison of their OPACs' presented at the VALE, NJ ACRL and NJLA

CUS Tenth Annual Users' Conference, January 2009. *http://valenews.files.wordpress.com/2009/01/opacs.ppt.*

Young, Jeffrey R. '5 Challenges for Open Source.' *Chronicle of Higher Education* (September 24, 2004). *http://chronicle .com/article/5-Challenges-for-Open-Source/18715/.*

Zhao, Luyin, and Fadi P. Deek. 'User Collaboration in Open Source Software Development.' *Electronic Markets* 14, no. 2 (June 2004): 89–103.

Index